T0215351

Pro iOS Testing

XCTest Framework for UI and Unit Testing

Avi Tsadok

Apress®

Pro iOS Testing: XCTest Framework for UI and Unit Testing

Avi Tsadok
Tel Mond, Israel

ISBN-13 (pbk): 978-1-4842-6381-5   ISBN-13 (electronic): 978-1-4842-6382-2
https://doi.org/10.1007/978-1-4842-6382-2

Copyright © 2020 by Avi Tsadok

Managing Director, Apress Media LLC: Welmoed Spahr
Acquisitions Editor: Aaron Black
Development Editor: James Markham
Coordinating Editor: Jessica Vakili

Distributed to the book trade worldwide by Springer Science+Business Media New York, 1 NY Plaza, New York, NY 10014. Phone 1-800-SPRINGER, fax (201) 348-4505, e-mail orders-ny@ springer-sbm.com, or visit www.springeronline.com. Apress Media, LLC is a California LLC and the sole member (owner) is Springer Science + Business Media Finance Inc (SSBM Finance Inc). SSBM Finance Inc is a **Delaware** corporation.

For information on translations, please e-mail booktranslations@springernature.com; for reprint, paperback, or audio rights, please e-mail bookpermissions@springernature.com.

Apress titles may be purchased in bulk for academic, corporate, or promotional use. eBook versions and licenses are also available for most titles. For more information, reference our Print and eBook Bulk Sales web page at http://www.apress.com/bulk-sales.

Any source code or other supplementary material referenced by the author in this book is available to readers on GitHub via the book's product page, located at www.apress.com/ 978-1-4842-6381-5. For more detailed information, please visit http://www.apress.com/ source-code.

Printed on acid-free paper

It is a big challenge to write a book while also being a full-time dad and an iOS developer.

Therefore, I would like to thank my family – my kids, Harel and Maya, and my loving wife, Tammy – who gave me the time and strength to sit down, investigate, dig, and write.

Without your unconditional support, this book would not exist.

Table of Contents

About the Author

Avi Tsadok is an accomplished iOS developer with almost a decade of experience. He currently heads mobile development at Any.do, a leading productivity app. He's also a regular contributor to "Better Programming" and has an active presence on Medium. Having written many iOS articles, he's decided to combine his passion for writing and developing by writing his first book.

About the Technical Reviewer

Felipe Laso is a Senior Systems Engineer working at Lextech Global Services. He's also an aspiring game designer/programmer. You can follow him on Twitter at @iFeliLM or on his blog.

CHAPTER 1

Introduction for Testing

If you don't like unit testing your product, most likely your customers won't like to test it either.

—Anonymous

Introduction

Software testing is a complementary process to your development flow. It may be the only way to monitor your work and your project over time, and as a result, it has a positive impact on how your project is built and how your code is written.

This book takes you from the very beginning of what software testing is, how to set up an excellent infrastructure, how to write a great, clean, testable code, and of course how to test your code in many ways and techniques.

In this first chapter, you will learn

- What is software testing

- How software testing is relevant for us, iOS developers

- Why it's so important

- What are the different main types of testing which we can use

© Avi Tsadok 2020
A. Tsadok, *Pro iOS Testing*, https://doi.org/10.1007/978-1-4842-6382-2_1

How to Read This Book

Although it's possible to read this book in chronological order, you don't have to follow that rule. There are some theoretical chapters that I recommend you start with, and for the practical chapters' part, you can read them in any order you want.

Even if you have a lot of experience with writing tests, I believe you can find new useful tips and exciting techniques to leverage your coding and testing skills.

There are plenty of code samples and examples throughout the book you can try yourself and even add them to your existing tests (if you have some).

What Is Software Testing?

Testing is a process aimed to retrieve information about the quality of an app, a feature, or a function. Developers and QA testers manage testing by running a program that examines your app code and decides if it's ready for production or if it's broken.

The testing process can investigate your app in several ways – product requirements, edge cases, performance, memory, different screens/devices, or integrations. In many cases, testing is a part of a continuous deployment service or integration, where it plays a significant role in an automatic deployment process to the App Store or TestFlight.

Software Testing in iOS

If you haven't written tests yet, the test target may look like an alien to you. To be aligned, take a look at the marked part in Figure 1-1.

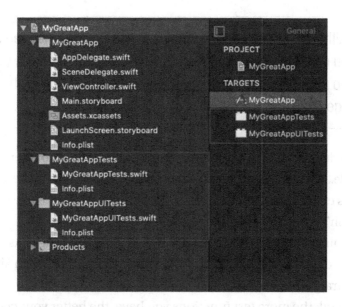

Figure 1-1. *Test targets in Xcode project*

Those are your project's test targets, and their primary mission is to help you monitor your code quality and performance. This is done using test functions when each of them is responsible for a specific use case.

A test function might look something like this:

```swift
func testPrimeNumberFunction() {
    // arrange
    let number = 7

    // act
    let result = MathService().isPrimeFunction(number: number)

    // assert
    XCTAssertTrue(result)
}
```

The preceding code is an example of a simple test function that checks if a function called isPrimeFunction() is working correctly.

Note   Although all the code examples in this book are written in Swift, you can write tests in Objective-C as well. But I'm sure you'll be able to understand most of my examples even if your Swift knowledge is poor.

As iOS developers, we write functions every day. Some of them are very simple, but some are incredibly complex. How can we make sure they perform as expected in different cases? Not only that – how can we make sure we don't break them over time as our project gets bigger?

If we consider ourselves professional developers, writing tests is not a "nice to have" task – it's a must. And if we write clean code, it can also be easy and straightforward.

In general, the more test functions you have, the better your code will be monitored and controlled.

This book aims not only to show you how to write great and useful tests. It also aims to influence your work culture.

Why Is Testing So Important?

If we want to dig deeper to understand the importance of testing in our projects, I can think of several reasons:

Refactoring – Some think that refactoring is a negative word that you do when you have a crisis or just a poorly written piece of code, but refactoring is a part of the developer's daily routine. When we write code, we do it based on a specific product assumption, SDK version, architecture, or our own experience and point of view. But things change rapidly in the technological (and especially in the mobile) world. We often find ourselves refactor parts of our code every few months and even less. When we write tests, we define how our code **behaves** and not how it is written. When we refactor, we need to keep the behavior of our code the same, and tests are our guiding angels for doing that. Not only that, tests actually "lock" the code at a specific quality level, and that's the way to make sure nothing is broken when we are making changes.

Check Ourselves – When we write a code or a feature, we need to make sure it works as required in all use cases and scenarios. Writing tests is a great way to check ourselves and make sure we covered what we need to answer the product requirements. It's also a great way to make sure we covered edge cases and use cases that are hard to test manually. For example, let's say we are working on a calendar app, and we need to test how our code performs when we have hundreds or even thousands of calendar events. Simulating a device with so many events is difficult and time-consuming, not to mention we need to run this simulation over and over again. Automating this process by writing a performance test is much more efficient and comfortable.

Prevent Regressions – Regressions in our code can happen not only when we refactor but also when we make small changes to a function, update the iOS version, or even install our app on a new device. The more we cover, the more chances we will catch regression bugs that could find their way into production. Sometimes it's hard to detect regressions in manual testing even if the QA member works with a very detailed test plan. For example, snapshot testing (explained later in the chapter) can detect minimal changes in the UI, and performance testing can detect changes in the speed of our code or memory usage. Also, it's tough to catch edge case issues when doing a standard manual regression testing, much harder than automated tests.

Better Code Quality – Tests can help us to come up with different use cases our code can bump into. Also, tests can help us measure our code resources (CPU/memory) usage and help to reduce it. Code coverage reports can help us detect untested parts of the code and can even bring up product issues we didn't think of just by the look on our code. But I believe that the best contribution tests do in terms of code quality is make us write better code and, more precisely, better architecture. To make our code testable, we need to write a cleaner, more modular, and protocol-oriented code, and this is a clean profit.

Documentation – I've got to admit – I hate writing technical documentation for my code. I write comments, but only because I have to. Otherwise, I won't understand what I meant to achieve even in the day after I wrote them. Tests are a great way to document your code. Think of it – you take a function and explain what is expected to happen when you call it with different parameters and in different situations. You won't find better documentation of your code than that.

What Can We Test?

Short answer – everything.

Long answer – depends.

If you have a look at the "Software Testing" page in Wikipedia, you can find around 20 different types of software testing techniques! But we are here to make our life simpler, so we'll discuss only some of these techniques which are mainly relevant for us as iOS developers.

Unit Tests – Unit tests are the bread and butter of testing. Unit Tests are responsible for testing small code pieces of your app, such as methods and functions. The unit tests are best for refactors and TDD (Test-Driven Development), and you should write as many of them.

The goal of a unit test is to test a specific function or method while ignoring and isolating the function from any possible side effect or outer state. Also, they are easy to write, run very fast, can be run in parallel, and writing them should be a natural step when developing a feature.

Integration Tests – If we said that unit tests live in isolation and that they focus on testing a specific method, there are cases when we need to test the integration between two or more layers of the app.

For example, sometimes we want to test the integration between the presenter/view model and the database layer. Integration tests are precisely for that. Some say integration tests are the most important tests you can have in your project even more than unit tests because, in the end, it doesn't matter how your unit tests perform, it's how they perform with each other.

UI Tests – UI Test refers to our app as a black box and uses the accessibility layer to activate it. The basic commands can be something like "press here" and "scroll there," and it's the closest thing to manual testing. Although UI Tests can perform as an edge-to-edge tests and can be very useful, they are expensive – they are harder to write and run much slower than unit tests. They can also break easily with every feature change. Also, since UI Tests can look only at the accessibility layer, they cannot produce a code coverage report. Therefore, they are not valid if you want to detect untested parts of your code.

Snapshot UI Testing – Snapshot testing is an addition to UI Testing. The way snapshot testing works is to take a snapshot of the screen or the view and compare it to a previously captured snapshot that represents the required one. The goal here is to identify any visual changes to the app, a task that is hard to do in any other way – for example, buttons' positions, font size changes, layout issues, and more.

Performance Testing – In every project, some methods are doing a massive job. These functions need optimization, and one of the best techniques is a performance test. Performance test runs your function several times; calculates the average CPU, memory usage, and running time; and decides if it passed or failed according to a minimum bar you can set in advance.

You don't have to cover every part of your project with all types of tests. For example, if we are dealing with view controllers or view models, we probably want to write **integration tests** to make sure everything works as expected when the user interacts with our app. If we need to deal with complex functions and classes, we are going to choose **unit tests** to cover our functions from all sides. And if these are heavily loaded functions, we can also add **performance** tests.

The secret is to create the right mix so that you could monitor your project from different angles and in various aspects.

Summary

We discussed what software testing is, how it is implemented in iOS, and why it's important. We also talked about different types of tests that are relevant for iOS development.

Now, it's time to pull our sleeves, set up our testing infrastructure in Xcode, and integrate it with our project.

CHAPTER 2

Setting Up Our Infrastructure

To an optimist, the glass is half full. To a pessimist, the glass is half empty. To a good tester, the glass is twice as big as it needs to be.

—Anonymous

Introduction

You cannot start writing tests without a deep understanding of how Xcode projects are built and how the testing layer integrates with it.

In this chapter, you will learn

1. The basic terms such as scheme, target, and project

2. How to customize your testing flows using schemes and test bundles

3. How to disable specific tests from running

4. How to take advantage of Xcode 11 great feature – Test Plan – to take your testing flows to the next level

© Avi Tsadok 2020
A. Tsadok, *Pro iOS Testing*, https://doi.org/10.1007/978-1-4842-6382-2_2

Basic Terms

To start testing your app, you need to understand some basic terms in Xcode and how your projects are built.

Let's start with one of the core Xcode terms – **Project**.

Project is a big file that maps all the files for your different products, including the build settings, assets, and more. It can stand alone, be included in a workspace, or be part of other projects.

> *An Xcode project is a repository for all the files, resources, and information required to build one or more software products. A project contains all the elements used to build your products and maintains the relationships between those elements. It contains one or more targets, which specify how to build products. A project defines default build settings for all the targets in the project (each target can also specify its own build settings, which override the project build settings).*
>
> —Apple Documentation

A project contains one or more definitions of products called "targets."

Target – A target represents a product to build and contains all the instructions on how to build it, including what files to compile, the build settings, build phases, code signing, and capabilities. A target doesn't have to be an "app." It can also be a framework/library, an extension (such as Today Widget), and, in our case, unit/UI test bundles that test other targets.

So, we understand that a target can be the app itself, and it can be the unit test product that tests the app. But how can we tell Xcode what test targets to run when we either start our test, build for the app store, or are just debugging and on what configuration?

That's what Schemes are for.

Schemes – Scheme connect targets with different scenarios (Build, Run, Test, Profile, Analyze, and Archive), and it also specifies what targets to run and on what configuration.

The best way to explain that is with Xcode, so let's start a new app called "My Weather" App.

"My Weather" App

To start a new Project, select File ➤ New ➤ Project.... A Popup dialog appears where you request to select a template for your new project. You can choose either iOS, watchOS, tvOS, macOS, or even a cross-platform project. Your project doesn't have to be an app; it can also be a framework or a static library (see Figure 2-1).

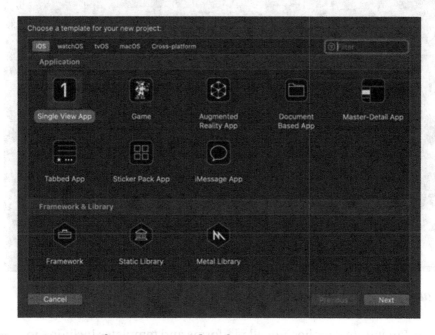

Figure 2-1. *Xcode project template box*

Note   Not every platform can be tested using Xcode tools. We'll discuss it later in this section.

11

After selecting the template, you are forwarded to a second dialog where you need to fill some details about your project. Some fields are required in order to continue (this is why the "Next" button is disabled). Take a look at the two options at the bottom (Figure 2-2), circled in red. Those options are suggested to you according to the platform and template you chose. If you mark them, Xcode creates an infrastructure for unit tests and UI tests. You can always do that later.

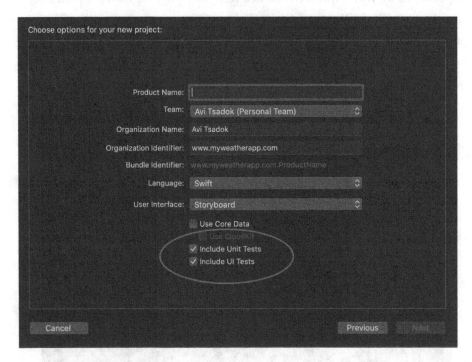

Figure 2-2. *New project setup box*

As I mentioned earlier, not all platforms and templates include those options. For example, as of this writing, you cannot add tests at all to an Apple Watch app. If you create a framework or a library, you can only add unit tests and not UI tests. Since our new cutting-edge and award-winning "My Weather" app is an iOS app, we can add both unit and UI tests.

After pressing the "Next" button, our project window is opened (Figure 2-3), and we can see the new test bundles under the list of targets. In the project navigator, we can see the two test bundles, unit and UI tests, as two groups of files. Those are the places where we save our coding test. For every target created, Xcode is creating a dedicated group of files in the project navigator.

Note There are "Groups" in the project navigator that represent links to actual folders, and there are "Groups" that represent logical folders. In this case, the two groups that were created refer to two folders in the project root folder.

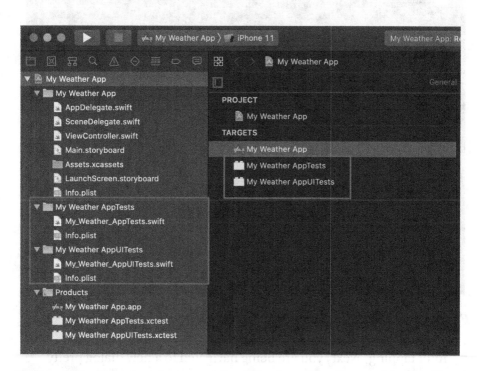

Figure 2-3. *Test targets appear both in the target list and in the file hierarchy*

Add Test Targets to an Existing Project

Of course, you don't have to create a new project to add UI and unit tests. It's straightforward to add tests to an existing project – just like adding any new target. To add a new test target, go to File ➤ New ➤ Target…. In the "Choose template" box that appears on the screen, look for UI Testing bundle or Unit Testing Bundle targets. You can take advantage of the search field in the top corner of the box (see Figure 2-4). Again, not all platforms have the option to add tests, so make sure the correct platform is selected.

Figure 2-4. *Adding test target to an existing project*

After tapping "Next", you are being navigated to a new dialog pretty similar to the new project dialog. Besides all the usual properties you need to fill there, such as bundle ID and name, the most important property is the "Target to be Tested." This target is the actual "product" (app or framework) that your new test bundle tests. "Target to be Tested" can also be changed later (see Figure 2-5).

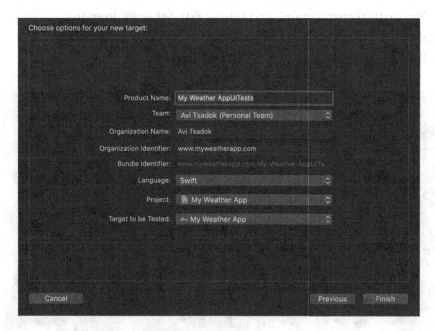

Figure 2-5. *Choose options for new test target*

Link Everything Together

At the beginning of the chapter, I mentioned the term "Schemes." Schemes let you define all the build configurations and options for different types of scenarios. You can have multiple schemes that can help you configure different scenarios and states for your app. For example, you can have a scheme that works with your development environment or a scheme that runs performance tests with an optimized code.

When you look at the top left corner of your Xcode window, next to the "stop" button, you can see the scheme menu and the selected scheme (see Figure 2-6).

Figure 2-6. *Scheme's popup menu in the toolbar*

Tap on the scheme name and select "Edit Scheme" from the popup menu. A box appears with the list of available actions and their configurations (Figure 2-7).

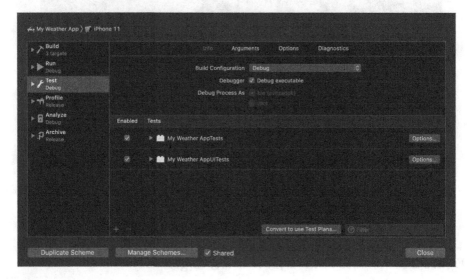

Figure 2-7. *Scheme edit box*

Let's go over the actions:

- **Build** – Compile your app without running it.

- **Run** – Build your app and run it either on a simulator or a device.

- **Test** – Build your app and run the enabled tests defined in the scheme.

- **Profile** – Run your app, and profile it with instruments.

- **Analyze** – Build the app with insights about your code.

- **Archive** – Build your app and create an IPA file from it to submit to the App Store.

In this chapter, I focus on the Test action. Tapping on the "Test" action displays four tabs: **Info**, **Arguments**, **Options**, and **Diagnostics**.

The Info Tab

Info – The Info tab contains general information about your test action in the scheme. The two most important settings here are the **Build Configuration** and the **list of tests**.

In Build Configuration, you can define if your tests run in Debug, Release, or your custom build configuration. There are cases where this is important – for example, sometimes you want to run a test against an optimized code for the App Store, or sometimes you want to run your tests with certain flags.

In the list of tests, you can see all the tests that are relevant for the executable product in the scheme. Remember, you can create as many tests as you want, but this is the place where you define **what** tests are executed when you test your app with this scheme.

Next to each test in the list, you have an enabled checkbox button that specifies if the list runs. On the right, you have a button named "options". Tap on it, and you can set **how** the test runs (again, only in this scheme) (see Figure 2-8).

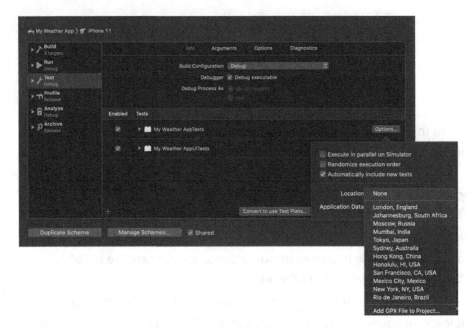

Figure 2-8. *Test options menu in scheme editor*

The options menu is unknown for many developers, and the button may look unimportant, but it holds extremely valuable settings.

Parallel Testing

The first option is the ability to **execute your tests in parallel**. Up until Xcode 9, you could only run your tests on one simulator at a time. In Xcode 9, Apple gave the ability to run your tests in multiple simulators. Xcode launches several simulators and runs the full test bundle on each one of them. Although this option speeds up the execution of the tests in case you want to run them on different devices, it doesn't speed up the test bundle itself.

Xcode 10 finally brings real parallel testing – it launches multiple test runners (Simulators), and each test runner receives a different test class from executing. The number of simulators is a derivative of the number of the available cores in the running machines.

Before you celebrate the parallel testing feature, you should be aware of the following:

- Parallel testing consumes a lot of **processing power**. If you want to take advantage of this feature, it's better to run it on a heavy machine as part of a continuous integration process.

- In parallel testing, each simulator receives different test classes. Different test classes mean that you **cannot create dependencies** in your tests. For example, testB() cannot rely on the success of the testA() and should run independently. Independent tests are important, especially in UI tests, when sometimes tests are expected to start in a particular state that is the result of another test.

- In case your tests are working against a server, running them in parallel can cause **a bottleneck in network requests** and as a result of that timeouts and test failures. In general, it's not the best practice to rely on a network in your tests, but sometimes you cannot avoid them in a certain integration and edge-to-edge scenarios.

Randomize Execution Order

In my opinion, "Randomize Execution Order" is a more significant thing than running your tests in parallel. While the latter influences the duration of your test run, the "randomize execution order" option influences the way you write tests.

Let me start with a popular hack many developers do when they write tests – in many test classes, you may see something like this:

```
func test01() {
    ...
}

Func test02() {
    ...
}
```

The hack the developer here tried to do is to make those tests run in a specific order. XCTest framework **runs tests by the lexicographic order**, and because 01 is bigger than 02, test01 runs before test02.

Running tests in a constant order can be convenient for some. It can help you start the test from the state the previous test ended and save you precious time when you want to test user flows. But this feature comes with a price – running tests in a constant order creates dependencies between your tests, and this makes your test suite much more fragile. Every small change can make one of the tests fail and, as a result of that, make the rest of the other tests to fail.

Tests supposed to run in isolation and not be dependent on an external or previous state of another test. The only way to ensure your tests are stable is to turn on the "Randomize Execution Order." Randomizing the test order forces you to write independent tests. It's better to rely on dependency injection and make your code more testable.

Location and Application Data

One of the most challenging tasks in integration and UI Tests is to simulate different conditions such as device location and application state. If we could use dependency injection in integration tests to somehow solve it, it's much harder to do that in UI Tests. A widespread use case for that is to simulate a particular condition for a bug or an edge case hard to debug.

In the scheme editor under the "test" action, we have two more options: **Location** and **Application Data**. Let's go over them.

Location

The Location option lets you simulate a specific geo-location for your test bundle or even a movement. Without the location feature, it is tough to simulate location changes or movement tracking.

The location popup menu in the editor scheme has a list of predefined locations like London, Moscow, New York, and more.

You don't have to settle for the predefined list, but you can create your own locations using a file format named "GPX." GPX (GPS Exchange) files contain location data such as longitude and latitude, waypoints, routes, and tracks. The basic format of GPX is XML, and you can create such a file in any text editor or online generator. Xcode itself has an option to create a GPX file, select from the menu File ➤ New ➤ File, and search for GPX in the dialog box (see Figure 2-9).

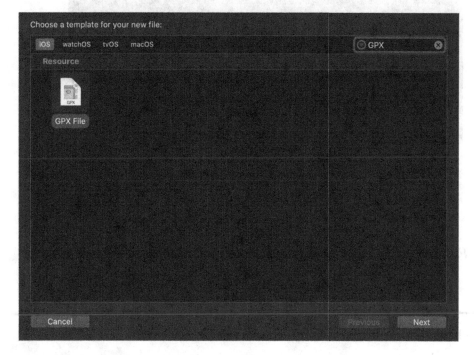

Figure 2-9. *Creating GPX file template*

The basic format of the GPX file should look something like this:

```
<gpx>
    <wpt lat="40.7484" lon="73.9857">
        <name>Empire States Building</name>
    </wpt>
</gpx>
```

After adding the file to your project, you can see the "Empire States Building" location in the list of locations (see Figure 2-10).

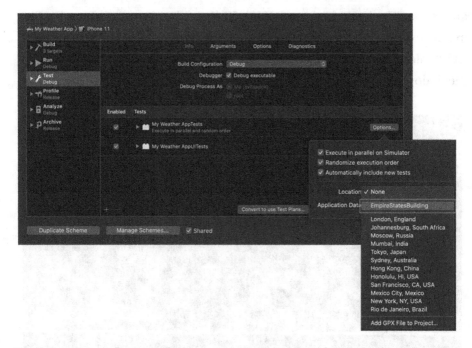

Figure 2-10. *Selecting the new custom location from the locations list*

GPX files can also contain movement. The way to do it is by adding multiple locations and timestamps so that Xcode can simulate the location changes according to the required pace.

```
<gpx>
  <wpt lat="40.606641" lon="-74.044835">
    <time>2020-03-01T16:25:12Z</time>
  </wpt>
  <wpt lat="40.608693" lon="-74.038514">
    <time>2020-03-01T16:25:17Z</time>
  </wpt>
  <wpt lat="40.610769" lon="-74.032217">
    <time>2020-03-01T16:25:26Z</time>
  </wpt>
</gpx>
```

Application Data

One of the neat features Xcode has is the ability to load the app in a specific app state, including persistent data, user defaults, and even cache. Loading the app with specific data is done using something called **XCAppData** file. XCAppData file is a files package that contains all the app data, including documents, Library, cache, and temporary file.

To get the XCAppData file, you need to make sure your device is connected to your Mac and go to Window ➤ Devices and Simulators. In the opened window, look for your connected device on the left and select it. Now you supposed to see the list of paired Apple Watches and installed apps (see Figure 2-11).

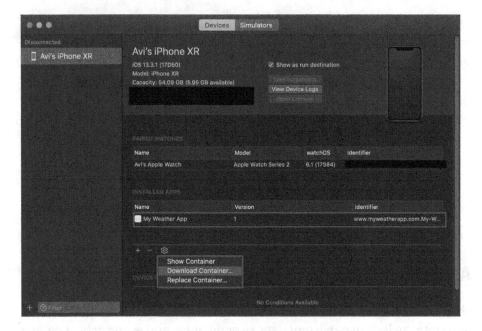

Figure 2-11. *Download application data container from your connected iPhone*

After selecting your app, you can download its app data container to your Mac. You should see a file with the following format:

`<bundleID>.<Date>.xcappdata`

For example:

`www.myweatherapp.com.My-Weather-App 2020-03-10 06/32.03.037.`
`xcappdata`

You should be aware of the fact that .xcappdata is a package, meaning it's a system directory displayed as a standard file and it contains additional files and directories. To open the package, right-click on the package in the Finder and select "Show Package Contents". After that, you can see the app data files hierarchy (see Figure 2-12).

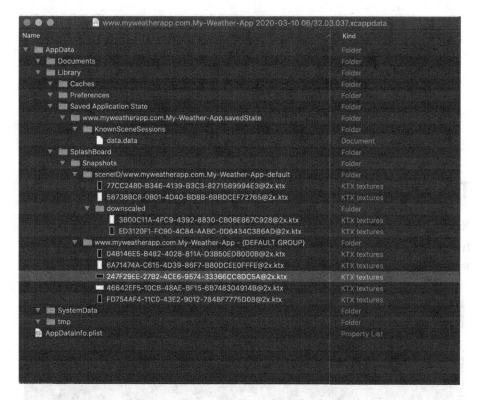

Figure 2-12. *Expanded app data package in the finder*

As you can see in Figure 2-12, the package contains all the app data that your device stores, including documents, temporary files, states, and even app screenshots the system uses for app switching user experience.

If you want to use the app data package (.xcappdata file) in your Xcode settings, you need to add it to your project.

Create a new group in your project, let's say "Tests Data," and add the package to that folder. Make sure the xcappdata doesn't belong to any target.

Note   Files that you want to use in your scheme such as GPX files and data packages should not be added to any target, not even your test target. If a file belongs to a certain target, it will be bundled with the final product and not only will increase the application size, but it can also reveal security and sensitive privacy information.

The Arguments Tab

Xcode has another neat and unknown features in their scheme editor, hidden under the arguments tab, called Launch Arguments and Environments Variables (see Figure 2-13).

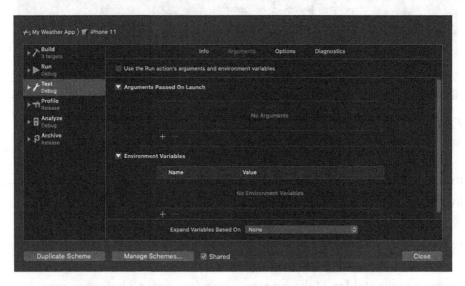

Figure 2-13. *The Arguments tab in scheme editor*

The Arguments tab lets you control the runtime of your app by setting arguments and variables that applied to the app only in this scheme.

Launch Arguments

Let's say we want to add an "In-App Purchase" capability to our "My Weather" app, and we want to run integration and UI tests when the user is already registered to our premium subscription.

The typical way many developers test their In-App Purchase is by returning "true" in the function that checks if the user is registered or not (look at the following code):

```
func isTheUserRegistered()->Bool {

return true

// The rest of the "real code", checking if the keychain
contains information about the user purchase

...

}
```

Returning "true" might work fine when you do your checks during development, but running tests like that may not be the right solution.

Fortunately, we can change values in runtime easily using the **"Arguments Passed on Launch"** list.

Arguments are a list of values passed to the app on launch and can be read in the code easily.

Your app can use arguments to run with specific flags without recompiling or using different targets. Arguments can be handy in testing because there are times when you want to mock different layers in your app, such as network, database, and more.

To add a new argument, go to the Arguments tab in the scheme editor, and under the list of arguments, tap on the plus button (see Figure 2-14).

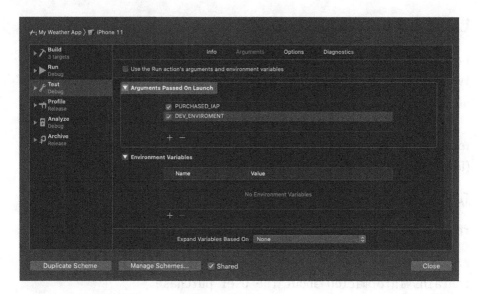

Figure 2-14. *List of added arguments*

If you don't want an argument to pass on launch, you don't need to delete it from the list; uncheck the checkbox near its name.

There are two similar ways to read the list of arguments in your code, **CommandLine** and **ProcessInfo**.

Look at the following code:

```
func application(_ application: UIApplication,
didFinishLaunchingWithOptions launchOptions: [UIApplication.
LaunchOptionsKey: Any]?) -> Bool {
        var purchasedIAP = CommandLine.arguments.
    contains("PURCHASED_IAP")

        // or we can use ProcessInfo
        purchasedIAP = ProcessInfo.processInfo.arguments.
    contains("PURCHASED_IAP")
```

```swift
    if purchasedIAP {
        // do something useful here...
    }

    return true
}
```

To clarify the differences between the two, **CommandLine** is part of Swift, and its primary goal is to read the command-line arguments, and, in this case, Arguments passed on launch.

ProcessInfo is part of foundation, and it contains information about the current process, including variables, host name, and also, just like CommandLine, the list of arguments.

For the goal of reading the arguments, you can use both of them.

Environment Variables

Just like many other development environments, iOS also has something similar called "Environment Variables." An environment variable is a collection of key–value which let you configure your app not just with a list of argument but also with values.

Adding an environment variable is just like adding an argument. Tap on the plus button under the variables list and add a new variable (see Figure 2-15).

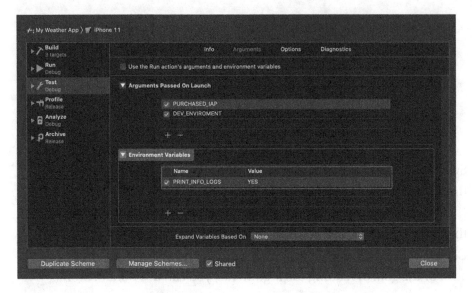

Figure 2-15. *Adding new environment variable to a scheme*

```
func application(_ application: UIApplication,
didFinishLaunchingWithOptions launchOptions: [UIApplication.
LaunchOptionsKey: Any]?) -> Bool {

    let printInfoLogs = ProcessInfo.processInfo.
    environment["PRINT_INFO_LOGS"]

    return true
}
```

Adding Environment Variables is also a great way to configure UI Tests by launching the app dynamically with different arguments each time. UI Tests will be covered later in this book.

The Options Tab

The options tab includes different settings related to your tests (see Figure 2-16).

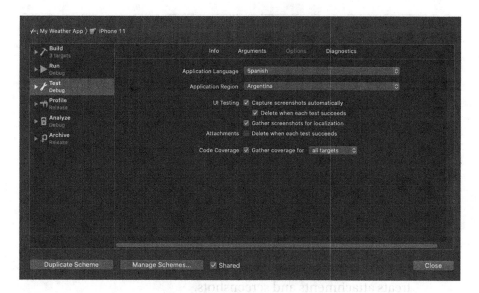

Figure 2-16. *The options tab in the scheme editor*

Let's go over those settings:

- **Application Language** – One of the biggest challenges
  of mobile development is localization – LTR vs. RTL and
  languages that contain long words and phrases. Not only
  can you set the device language using that option, but
  you can also simulate different text directions and even
  double the length of the texts to detect UI layout glitches.

Figure 2-17. *The Application Language settings*

- **Application Region** – Different regions mean different
  date formats, different currencies, and different
  measuring systems. By choosing the application region,
  you can test your app as if the device is in another region.

Note   While it's a convenience to set different languages and regions to test functions, sometimes it can be not very easy when you want to run a unit test multiple times for different regions. Later in this book, I will cover how to do this without the need of scheme options but with excellent and testable architecture.

- **UI Testing** – Unlike unit and integration tests, getting the reason why the UI test failed can be a little tricky. Screenshots and attachments are the best way to display the failure reason and the app state at that time. The UI Testing options let configure how your test treats attachments and screenshots.

Figure 2-18. *Application Language and Application Region settings*

- **Code Coverage** – We discussed code coverage in Chapter 1. Without marking this option, Xcode won't collect code coverage during your tests.

The Diagnostics Tab

The diagnostics tab is almost similar to the diagnostics tab you can find under "Run". This tab contains tools that can help determine issues with your app while running your tests, such as memory corrupts and thread issues (see Figure 2-19).

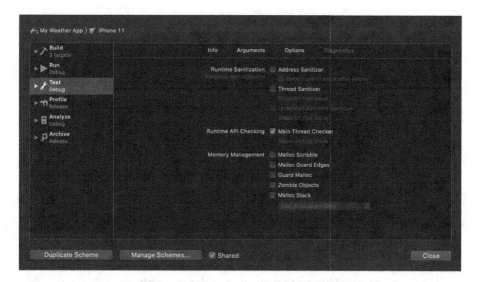

Figure 2-19. *The Diagnostics Tab in the Scheme Editor*

Since those tools are not explicitly related to testing, I will go over them in short.

My recommendation for you is to learn those tools deeper if you want to investigate your issues better.

- **Address Sanitizer** – This tool, introduced in Xcode 7, can help you debug memory corruption issues with your app. Those issues don't have to be just crashes – it can be general bugs as well. The combination of Address Sanitizer and Unit Tests can be beneficial under challenging bugs, but you should be aware of two downsides regarding this tool:

  - Address Sanitizer is much more relevant for C and Objective-C code rather than Swift.

- Address Sanitizer comes with a cost – your app consumes 2x–3x more memory and 2x–5x more CPU power when enabled. While this may seem not a big issue when running tests, it can be an issue when running performance tests when you measure critical metrics such as CPU time and memory.

- **Thread Sanitizer** – Thread Sanitizer is another LLVM-based tool that can help you detect data race between threads, which can cause unpredictable behavior. Just like Address Sanitizer, Thread Sanitizer doesn't come without a cost – memory usage increases by 5x–10x, and CPU performance increases by 2x–20x. Also, you cannot run Thread Sanitizer on a device, only on simulators.

- **Main Thread Checker** – One of the first rules every developer learns when he starts developing for iOS is never to run UI operations in the background but only on the main thread. Main Thread Checker stops your app at the point when it detects UI operation done on any background thread. This can be great in UI testing when you entirely run your app and feel safe all of your operations are on the right thread as they should.

- **Malloc Scribble** – Helps you debug reference counting cycles by filling freed memory with predefined values and by that to get more accurate results in memory graph.

- **Malloc Guard Edges** – Add guard pages before and after large allocations.

- **Guard Malloc** – Helps you catch common memory problems such as buffer overruns and use-after-free.

- **Zombie Objects** – One of the most popular tools Xcode has to offer. Zombie Objects are objects that were released (reference count 0) and replaced by a zombie object. Zombie Objects can help you track variables by keeping a copy of them in memory.

Exclude Test Classes

You might be wondering, "There's a whole chapter describing the importance of tests. Why on earth we want to exclude some of them from our test bundles?"

Well, in big, old projects, there are situations where tests may fail or even are not compiled because of a massive structural change, and we wish to disable them from running temporarily.

Xcode lets you not only disable test bundles in your scheme settings but also disable specific test classes and even test functions.

There are three ways of doing that – from scheme editor, from the Test Navigator, and by renaming test functions.

Disable Tests from the Scheme Editor

If you want to disable a test in a specific scheme, unchecking it from the scheme editor is one way of doing that. Open the scheme editor, and under Test ➤ Info, expand the test bundle in the list of test bundles (see Figure 2-20).

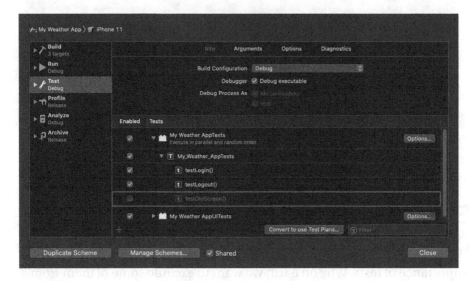

Figure 2-20. *Disable specific test from the scheme editor*

Remember, the disabling test only disables it from the specific scheme, so make sure you are doing this operation on the desired scheme.

Also, you can disable the whole class by unchecking the checkbox near the class name or disable the whole test bundle by unchecking the checkbox near the test bundle name.

Disable Tests from the Test Navigator

Maybe the easiest way to disable a test is from the Test Navigator or the code editor.

From the Navigator pane, open the Test Navigator by selecting it or pressing ⌘-6.

Search the test you want to disable and right-click it (see Figure 2-21).

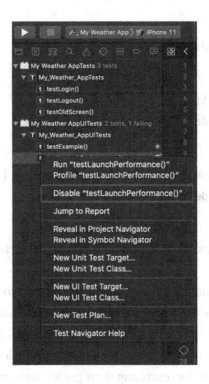

Figure 2-21.

Select "Disable <name of the test>" from the popup menu. Disabling can be done for classes and test bundles as well. In case the test is already disabled, you can re-enable it again from the same menu.

This approach also works from the code editor – right-click the function of the class you want to disable and choose "Disable <name of the function>".

Disable Tests by Renaming Them

Another way to disable tests is by renaming them with some prefix other than "test". Since Xcode runs only test functions that start with "test", changing the prefix disables them.

```
func testLogin() {
    // test code
}

func testLogout() {
    // test code
}

func disable_due_refactor_testOldScreen() {
    // test code
}
```

In the preceding example, Xcode ignores the third function since we changed its prefix.

In general, renaming test functions is considered to be an anti-pattern, and you should follow the natural way of disabling the tests using the scheme editor or the Test Navigator. The renaming test function does have one advantage, though – you can set a different prefix for a different reason and then relocate them by searching their prefix. Renaming a function name is a convenient way when you're doing a big refactor and want to disable tests by categories.

Note   It would be best if you never left disabled tests forever. Having disabled tests should be a temporary situation only; it exists only to let our project compile. Those tests are there for a reason; remember that.

How Many Test Bundles to Create?

The number of test bundles changed from project to project, but if I have to choose one rule of thumb, I would say it's a separation of concerns. If you remember from the first chapter, there are several types of tests:

UI tests; unit tests, which include BDD and TDD; integration tests, and performance tests. Unit tests can be used both for BDD, TDD, Integration, and performance. UI Tests can be used for BDD. But it's a best practice to separate your test bundles according to your company flows. For example, if you have a significant new feature in development, you can create a test bundle for it, and it will be easier to run it only when needed.

Here are some ideas on how to separate your tests:

- Separate BDD from TDD.

- Separate regression tests from sanity and feature testing.

- Separate significant features from the others.

Separating your project to different test bundles can give you necessary flexibility in the future and can help maintain your test's infrastructure and control it.

Test Plans

We saw that schemes are great tools to configure your test runs. Now let's say you want to run your tests several times with a different configuration each time. Different configurations mean you need to either create different schemes and run them one by one or change your current test scheme configuration each time before you run it.

Fortunately, Apple introduced a new feature in Xcode 11 called "Test Plans" which aims to solve exactly that – running the same test suite multiple times but with a different configuration.

Test Plans to Make Your Life Easier

Test Plans take the power of the test run customization in Xcode to the next level by giving you the flexibility to run your tests with different settings multiple times. Each Test Plan can test different issues that you may have in your app. Maybe the most common problem developers have with their apps is localization – you can create a test plan dedicated to localization and run the same tests over and over again but with different languages and regions.

The same goes for almost every option you currently have in your scheme editor.

Create Your First Test Plan

The easiest way to start with the Test Plan's feature is right from the scheme editor. Go to your scheme editor, and in the Test action, you can find a button called "Convert to user Test Plans..." under the list of your test bundles (see Figure 2-22).

Figure 2-22. Scheme editor, "Convert to use Test Plans..." button

After tapping the button, you'll have a dialog when you need to choose how to convert your new scheme to use test plans instead (see Figure 2-23).

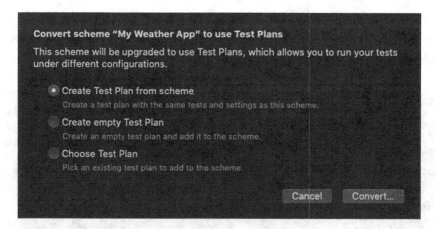

Figure 2-23. Converting a scheme to use test plans

Let's talk about those three options:

- **Create Test Plan from Scheme** – This option creates a Test Plan based on the current scheme configuration. After all, the test plan configuration is similar to the scheme test configuration, and it's easy to create a new test plan with the old options. "Creating Test Plan from Scheme" is the recommended option for the first test plan of your project.

- **Create Empty Test Plan** – Creates a new test plan template regarding the scheme test configuration.

- **Choose Test Plan** – Add an existing test plan to the scheme. It can be a test plan you created from scratch (Test Plan is an XML file; you can create it with any text editor), but in most cases, this option comes in handy when you create a new scheme and want to connect it to an existing test plan from another scheme.

After creating the test plan, it is saved to your project, and the Xcode upgrades the scheme to use Test Plans instead of the old Info/Arguments/ Options/Diagnostics screen we covered earlier (see Figure 2-24).

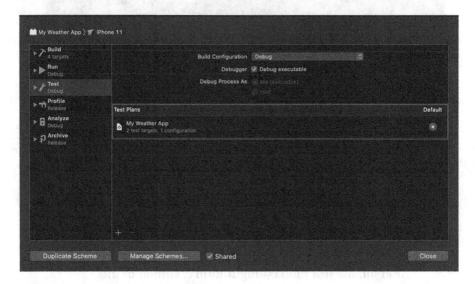

Figure 2-24. *Scheme converted to use test plans in its tests*

Scheme can contain multiple test plans. In each test plan, you can see how many test targets it runs and how many different configurations it has.

When you select "Test" for this scheme (Command + U), the test plan, which is marked as default, runs according to its configuration.

Test Plan Configurations

If we open our new "My Weather App.xctestplan" file that was added to our project, we could see it's just a simple XML file:

```
{
  "configurations" : [
    {
      "id" : "C9003BF5-4AD2-45D6-BB60-30C721C0D075",
      "name" : "Configuration 1",
      "options" : {

      }
    }
  ],
  "defaultOptions" : {
    "codeCoverage" : false
  },
  "testTargets" : [
    {
      "target" : {
        "containerPath" : "container:My Weather App.xcodeproj",
        "identifier" : "9032DE112411A30D00F8F02D",
        "name" : "My Weather AppTests"
      }
    },
    {
      "target" : {
        "containerPath" : "container:My Weather App.xcodeproj",
        "identifier" : "9032DE1C2411A30D00F8F02D",
        "name" : "My Weather AppUITests"
      }
    }
  ],
  "version" : 1
}
```

Although we are not supposed to edit the .xctestplan file directly, we can learn that Test Plan is quite simple. It contains an array of configurations and an array of test targets. Test Plan also has a default options section in case they are not set in the configurations themselves.

Tapping on the test plan in the project navigator will open the test plan edit screen (see Figure 2-25).

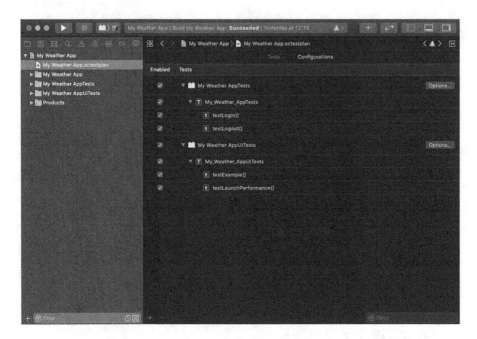

Figure 2-25. *Test Plan edit screen*

As you can see, you can enable/disable test bundles, classes, and functions just like you can do in your scheme editor. If you notice, you also have a new tab named "Configurations". If the "Tests" define **what** your test plan runs, "Configurations" define **how** your test plan runs it. A test plan configuration contains a list of values like location, region, and more, very similar to the options you had in your scheme editor. The significant difference here is that you can create as many configurations as you want (see Figure 2-26).

Figure 2-26. *Test Plan configuration*

The test plan in Figure 2-26 tries to test the app in different localization. Localization is one example of how a Test Plan can be useful. You can have several test plans that can handle different issues such as memory and performance issues, localization, and more. Whenever you run a test plan, Xcode runs the selected tests one time **for each configuration**, and there's no limit on the number of configurations you can create. This is something tough to do without using a test plan.

Note   There's no need to go over the list of options in a test plan configuration, as it was covered earlier in this chapter.

If you want to disable a test configuration from running, right-click the configuration name and select "Disable".

Running Your Test Plans

Because we added a new layer of complexity, let's try to simplify what we have learned till now and how everything is linked together (see Figure 2-27).

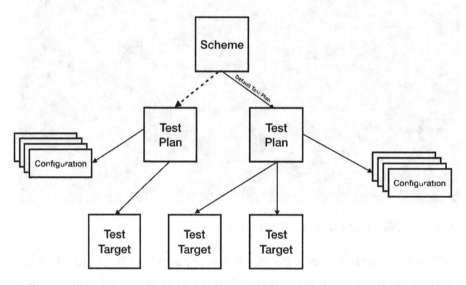

Figure 2-27. *How Scheme, Test Plans, Tests, and configurations are linked together*

As you can see from the preceding diagram, a scheme can have multiple test plans, but when you run a test, only one of them executes.

To run the test plan selected for the scheme, press Command + U or run it from the Test Navigator.

Running Only One Configuration

As already mentioned, a test plan can contain many configurations. While it's important to run them all as part of a continuous integration flow, during development, you may want to run just one configuration to save precious time.

In that case, it's effortless to run the test plan according to a specific configuration.

To do that, right-click the desired test function/class/ bundle and select the desired configuration (see Figure 2-28).

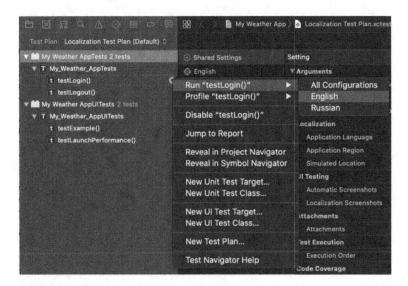

Figure 2-28. *Run only English configuration*

Summary

From now on, schemes, targets, and test plans should be your best friends. Knowing them well can help you adapt your tests to your daily development flow, and it's a prerequisite for the next chapters where we are going to learn how to write tests in all colors and forms.

Are you ready to start testing?

CHAPTER 3

Writing Tests – The Basics

Pay attention to zeros. If there is a zero, someone will divide by it.

—Dr. Cem Kaner

Introduction

In the previous chapter, we have learned how to set up our infrastructure for testing. It seems we are ready to write. But, even when your code is excellent, with pure functions and dependency injection, we need to learn the basics of how to write proper tests that we can maintain over time.

In this chapter, you will learn

- What exactly are **unit tests**

- What are the **XCTest** framework and **XCTestCase** class

- How to **configure** your target and your test bundle to work together

- About the **XCTestCase life cycle** and how it works under the hood

- How to write a **simple unit test** method and how it is **built**

© Avi Tsadok 2020
A. Tsadok, *Pro iOS Testing*, https://doi.org/10.1007/978-1-4842-6382-2_3

- What **assertions** we have and how we can create our **assertions**

- How to test **asynchronous** operations

What Exactly Are Unit Tests?

Unit Test is a function that tests a specific piece of code and assets in the case the results of the test are not according to the requirements.

When you try to add a test, you have two options – Unit Tests and UI Tests. In this step, "Unit Test" is just a tool that can help you create different kinds of tests – integration tests, performance tests, regressions tests, and more.

But "Unit Tests" in the traditional way of meaning is a software testing method.

The goal of the unit test method is to check a code, isolated, without examining its side effects on other layers or objects.

Unit Tests have several characteristics:

- They should run **fast**. There shouldn't be any real heavy loaded code in Unit Tests or integration with a server or a database. A normal test suite should run in seconds. If this is not the case, you should check if all the tests you created are unit tests.

- Unit Tests are **easy to build**. You shouldn't work hard to set up a unit test. If it takes too much effort on your side, maybe it's not a unit test or maybe your code is not testable enough. In this case, go over the previous chapter to learn how to improve your code testability.

- Unit Tests need the ability to run **in parallel**. Isolation is the key here. Running in parallel is the best way to ensure your unit tests don't have any unknown side effects that can influence not just other tests but also your code in an unpredictable way.

– Unit Tests are in charge of checking the **behavior of a method or even a specific piece of code**. Unit Tests are not supposed to check how layers in your app work together, find memory leaks, or make sure your code runs fast enough.

You should write as many unit tests as you can as part of your daily development routine. If you write a readable and clear code, it's not supposed to be a difficult task.

Note   Unit Tests are not TDD, and TDD is not Unit Tests. Developers often mix those terms. Unit Tests are **what** you test, and TDD is **when** you test it. In TDD, you write your unit test before the actual code, and unit tests are integrated in this process.

XCTest and XCTestCase

XCTest is the framework used to write tests for your app. It comes as part of your Xcode, and there is no additional setup required to start writing tests.

XCTest is also the name of the abstract class for creating and executing tests, both Unit Tests and UI Tests. To create a new test class, we are going to make use of XCTest's subclass – XCTestCase.

XCTestCase

When we want to create a new test class, we need to subclass XCTestCase. In unit tests, we usually want to create one test class to handle one "regular" class in our project. The recommended name can be the name of the tested class with the addition of the word "tests." For example, for a class named "LoginHandler", we can create a test class named "LoginHandlerTests". This can help us understand exactly what this class tests and also prevent redeclaration of the same class name by mistake.

Adding a New XCTestCase Subclass

To add a new test case, go to File ➤ New ➤ File and select "Unit Test Case Class" (see Figure 3-1).

Figure 3-1. *Adding new Unit Test Case Class*

After tapping "Next", give a name for the test class and choose its location in your project just like any other file.

Notice that, in the last step, you need to choose the test target this test class belongs to (Figure 3-2) – this is extremely important since test classes cannot be part of your executable target.

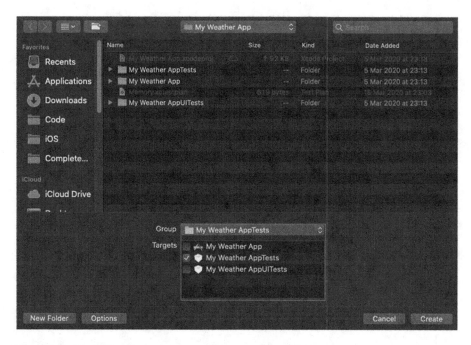

Figure 3-2. *Selecting a target for your test class*

Our First Test Class

Congratulations, it's a test class!

Look at how our new test class looks like:

```
import XCTest // 1

class DemoTests: XCTestCase { // 2

    override func setUpWithError() throws { // 3
        // Put setup code here. This method is called before
        the invocation of each test method in the class.
    }
```

```
override func tearDownWithError() throws { // 4
    // Put teardown code here. This method is called after
    the invocation of each test method in the class.
}

func testExample() throws { // 5
    // This is an example of a functional test case.
    // Use XCTAssert and related functions to verify your
    tests produce the correct results.
}

func testPerformanceExample() throws { // 6
    // This is an example of a performance test case.
    self.measure {
        // Put the code you want to measure the time of here.
    }
}
}
```

Let's go over it together:

1. **import XCTest** – In order to subclass XCTestCase and add it to the test runner, we need to import the XCTest framework just like any other framework we want to use.

2. **class DemoTests: XCTestCase** – Always make sure you are subclassing from XCTestCase.

3. **setUpWithError()** – This method runs **before** every test method execution. It will be explained later in this chapter.

4. **tearDownWithError()** – This method runs **after** every test method execution. It also will be explained later in this chapter.

5. **testExample()** – This is our first unit test example. Currently, it's empty.

6. **testPerformanceExample()** – This is a performance test example. It will be explained later in this book.

Enable Testability

Before we move on and add more tests, we need to make sure everything is linked up correctly in our project.

Your test code is *not* part of your executable. It's a different module in your Xcode project, and for your tests to have access to your app code, you need to take care of access privileges.

But don't worry; there is a fairly simple flag to help you with the access privileges problem, and it's called "Enable Testability".

When you go to your executable target, under "Build Settings", search for "Enable Testability". Setting this flag to "YES" gives your test targets access to code. Take a look at Figure 3-3.

Figure 3-3. *Set "Enable Testability" to YES*

One thing we notice here is that this flag is set to NO in release configuration. One reason for that is that we do not need access to the executable code since we usually don't test our app in release configuration. The more important reason for that is that this option prevents code optimization, which is used in release configuration and is not suitable for your tests and for debugging.

@testable

So now after we took care of the settings in the executable side, we need to import the executable target to the test class.

On the top of the file, just above the class declaration, we add a new attribute called "@testable":

```
import XCTest

@testable import My_Weather_App

class My_Weather_AppTests: XCTestCase {

    // testing code
}
```

What @testable does and why do we need it? First, lets recall the five access levels in Swift:

- **Public** – Anyone can access within the module and in external code that imports the module.

- **Open** – It is same as **Public,** but it is possible to subclass it from any module and not just the original class module.

- **Internal** – Access is prohibited outside the module. The internal access level is the **default** level for classes and methods.

- **Fileprivate** – Access is only from the current file.

- **Private** – Access is only from the same class or struct.

If you notice, the default access for classes and methods is **internal**. Because Unit Tests require full access to your code outside the module, we may have a problem here assuming your access level for most classes and methods is set to the default one.

What @testable does is to elevate access levels in the imported module. Members marked as **Public** now behave as **Open,** and members marked as **Internal** behave as **Public**.

Note   There are some discussions in the Swift developers' community about @testable. Some claim @testable attribute is a "hack" who tries to overcome the access level issue in testing. Those who claim that, say that since it's a "hack," why not give private and fileprivate public access level as well?

CocoaPods and Testing Targets

Many projects today use Dependency Manager to integrate with external libraries and frameworks. One of the most popular managers is CocoaPods with over 72,000 libraries, and it's used in more than three million apps.

One of the tasks CocoaPods does when linking a new framework is to update the *header search path* according to the new integrated frameworks.

If you want to use those libraries directly in your test target, you need to add your test target to the Podfile file, like this:

```
target "My_Weather_AppTests" do
  inherit! :search_paths
  pod 'Fabric', '1.10.2'
  pod 'Firebase'
end
```

Adding pods to the test target is something developers usually forget during test writing, so the key to remember that is to treat the test target as a separate app. Everything you want to use, you need to link it to your test target, just as you would do in your executable target.

XCTestCase Life Cycle

XCTestCase life cycle is a little bit different than what you would expect in standard Swift classes. Because test cases are part of a test runner, the test runner calls the test case methods in a specific timing, suitable for testing.

Class Method setUp()

When a new test class starts its run (it's more accurate to say that we are "adding the test case to the test runner"), the first method to be called is the setup() method in the class level. You don't have to override it, of course, but this method is called once for all the tests in the class. setup() method is the place for you to do some initial setup for your tests, such as creating a database or setting up a mock server:

```
override class func setUp() {
    super.setUp()

    // runs once before all the tests begin
}
```

Method setUpWithError () throw

After class method setup(), XCTest locates all the methods in the class that start with "test" **and** don't have any arguments.

For each one of those methods, XCTest calls setUpWithError() function before it runs the test method itself. This is the place where you can prepare any instance variables you have instead of duplicating those steps in every test method.

Also, an instance method setup() is called after each setUpWithError() call.

You might notice that setUpWithError() method is a throwing method. This is a welcome addition in Xcode 11.4, since a lot of code that is done at this method is a throwing code, for example:

```
override func setUpWithError() throws {
    networkResponse = try buildResponseFromJSON(filename :
    "response.json")
}
```

If setUpWithError() throws, it means that the test that follows it will fail as well.

Test Methods

After setting up the state for the test, XCTest runs the test method and asserts if needed. XCTest considers a method to be a test method if all the following conditions exist:

- It belongs to a subclass of XCTestCase.

- Its name starts with "test".

- The method doesn't have any arguments.

A test method passes if it doesn't have any failed assertions or crashes. We'll talk about how to write test methods later in this chapter.

Teardown Block

If your test method changes some state or has a specific side effect you want to clean up, you can add a teardown block that runs at the end of the test:

```
func testExample() throws {
    // creating a temporary file

    addTeardownBlock {
        // removing the temporary file
    }
}
```

You can add as many teardown blocks as you want, and it's explicit for changes made at this function only. To create a teardown code that runs after each method, you need to override the **tearDownWithError()** method.

Method tearDownWithError() throw

tearDownWithError method runs after each test method whether it failed or passed. We use this method to clean up any side effect your test method might have caused, and in most cases, it should be the inverse function of setUpWithError() method.

For example, if you opened up a connection to SQLite in setUpWithError(), this is the place to close it:

```
override func tearDownWithError() throws {
    try super.tearDownWithError()

    // clean up any side effects caused by setupWithError()
}
```

Just like setUpWithError() and setup(), tearDownWithError() is called before "tearDown()". They are both valid so that you can use them in your projects.

Class Method tearDown()

Class method tearDown() is the parallel closing function of the class
method "setup()". It runs at the end of all tests and is used to clean up any
setup code you did before the tests started to run:

```
override class func tearDown() {
    super.tearDown()

    // runs at the end of all tests in the class, and is
    used to clean up any side effect the class method
    setup() might have caused.
}
```

How It All Fits Together

Confused? Well, that sounds normal. But setting up the initial state for a
test and cleaning it up afterward are crucial steps to achieve stability in
your test run.

This is why I created Figure 3-4 to show you how it looks from above.

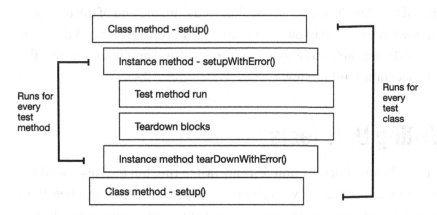

Figure 3-4. *XCTestCase life cycle*

XCTest Creates an XCTestCase Instance for Every Test Method

Some may think that before a test case class starts its execution, XCTest creates an instance of this class and just runs all the tests one by one. While that makes sense in standard classes, this is not the case in XCTest classes.

When Xcode starts its test suite, it actually creates an XCTestCase instance **for every test method** and adds it to its test runner queue **before** the test execution even begins.

Let's say you have a test class named "LoginTests" with four different test methods. When the test run begins, XCTest creates four instances of LoginTests class, one for each test method, and adds them to the test runner. Those four instances get deallocated at the end of the run, only after all the other tests finished their execution.

And this is important because it can give you a sense about how states are managed during the test run execution. For example, you cannot share an instance variable value across different test methods, since each one of those methods has its own class instance.

And regarding memory management, you need to remember that none of the class instances get deallocated until the end of the test run. This means you need to pay attention to what you are doing in the setup and tearDown methods and make sure to release and reset any data that can affect other test methods.

Writing Unit Tests

As I said before, not only unit tests are fast to run, but they also need to be written fast. But don't worry; you don't have to invent the wheel here – there are particular pattern and structure on how to write unit tests. If you'll keep a constant pattern, not only will they be easy to write but also readable.

Unit Test Anatomy

Take a look at the following code:

```
func testGetSpeedLimit_private_expect110() {
    // arrange
    car.type = .private

    // act
    let speedLimit = car.getSpeedLimit()

    // assert
    XCTAssertEqual(speedLimit, 110)
}
```

As you can see, in a unit test, we have three steps **A**rrange, **A**ct, **A**ssert, or in short AAA. We can also call it GWT (**G**iven-**W**hen-**T**hen). Some developers prefer AAA since its terminology is closer to the code level, and some prefer GWT for easier communication with the business level.

But in the bottom line, it doesn't matter. The idea stays the same:

- **Arrange/Given** – Do all the setup for the test here. Connect dependencies, set properties, and allocate variables. Remember what we learned about the life cycle. If it's something you do in every test method, consider moving it to the setup() method to save yourself code duplication.

- **Act/When** – This is the place when you execute the function you want to test. In this stage, it is best practice to save the value you want to verify against your requirements in a local variable.

- **Assert/Then** – The final setup is the actual validation of the test. In this step, you check if the test fulfills the expectation, generally by asserting (we will discuss it later).

Separating your test method into three steps makes your testing code much more readable and easier to understand.

Assertions

There is a long list of assertions XCTest supports. In all assertions, you have the option to include a formatted error message to help you understand what the failed test is and the reason for the failure is. This is especially important when running tests from the command line or CI/CD environment, but also helpful from Xcode itself.

Table 4-1. *List of XCTest Assertions*

Name	Description
XCTFail	Unconditionally fails the test
XCTAssertNil	Failure when the passed object is not nil
XCTAssertNotNil	Failure when the object is nil
XCTAssertEqual	Failure when expressions are not equal
XCTAssertNotEqual	Failure when expressions are equal
XCTAssertNotEqualObjects	Failure when objects are not equal
XCTAssertNotEqualObjects	Failure when objects are equal
XCTAssertNoThrow	Failure when expression throws expression
XCTAssertGreaterThan	Failure when the first object is not greater than the second object
XCTAssertLessThan	Failure when the first object is not smaller than the second object
XCTAssertLessThanOrEqual	Failure when the first object is greater than the second object
XCTUnwrap	Failure when the given expression tries to unwrap and returns nil

You may wonder, "Why do I need to learn the full assertions list? I can just use XCTAssertTrue."

So basically, you are right. If you use XCTAssertTrue and pass the condition you want, this will actually do the job.

But take a look at Figure 3-5.

```
func testEquatable() {
    let x = 1
    let y = 2
    XCTAssertTrue(x == y)                    ⊗  English: XCTAssertTrue failed
}
```

Figure 3-5. XCTAssertTrue failure in Xcode

Do you see the problem? Sure, "x == y" is not "true". But we didn't want to check a Boolean expression; we wanted to check if **two objects are equal**.

Now let's change it to **XCTAssertEqual** (Figure 3-6).

```
func testEquatable() {
    let x = 1
    let y = 2
    XCTAssertEqual(x, y)  ⊗  English: XCTAssertEqual failed: ("1") is not equal to ("2")
}
```

Figure 3-6. XCTAssertEqual failure in Xcode

As you can see, using the right assertion can help you get a descriptive failure message free of charge.

Creating a Custom Assertion

Believe it or not, there are cases when the existing assertions are not the precise and convenient tool for validating your tests.

Luckily, there's a way of creating your custom assertions and making your testing code much cleaner.

Here are some of the use cases that can make you consider writing your own custom assertion:

- **Duplicate Assertion Code** – Let's say you want to validate an object configuration, and you need to check a few properties. You can either use one big assertion that checks several values (an ugly solution) or use multiple assertions which is not an elegant solution either. The bottom line is when you see a repeated use of assertion sequence, you should consider a custom assertion.

- **When Your Assertion Code Is Too Big** – If you need to parse a JSON every time and check a certain value or if you need to analyze a string or to do some calculation, write your own assertion. When you feel that the last part of your test (the "Assert" or "Then" part) is too big and can be a good fit to a function of its own, this is a sign you should create a custom assertion.

- **When Your Assertion Doesn't Speak the Right Language** – If you are checking that an email address is valid or the string contains only one "@", or maybe you want to check if a date object is in a certain month or year. Sure, you can use a standard assertion for that, but the standard assertions don't speak the "same language." "Bigger than," "Equal," or "isTrue" is fine to use, but for a more stylish way, it is better to use your assertion to do those validations.

I'm In. How to Write My Own Assertion?

The basic method of writing your own assertion is, well, a new method in your tests.

66

Let's look at the following example:

```
func testPersonFetcher_getPersonByID_checkProperties() {
    // arrange
    PersonDataBase().insertNewPerson(newPerson:
    Person(firstName: "Tyler", lastName: "Butler"))
    let personFetcher = PersonFetcher()

    // act
    let person = personFetcher.getPerson(byID: "me")!

    // assert
    XCTAssertEqual(person.firstName, "Tyler")
    XCTAssertEqual(person.lastName, "Butler")
}
```

In this test method, we are fetching a "Person" object and check its first and last name. Now let's say for the sake of our example that we want to bundle those two assertions to one function that checks both first and last name. We can create a function that gets three arguments, the "Person" object, first name, and last name, as strings and run those two assertions:

```
func checkPersonValues(person: Person, firstName : String,
lastName : String) {
    XCTAssertEqual(person.firstName, firstName)
    XCTAssertEqual(person.lastName, lastName)
}

func testPersonFetcher_getPersonByID_checkProperties() {
    // arrange
    PersonDataBase().insertNewPerson(newPerson:
    Person(firstName: "Tyler", lastName: "Butler"))
    let personFetcher = PersonFetcher()
```

```
// act
let person = personFetcher.getPerson(byID: "me")!

// assert
checkPersonValues(person: person, firstName: "Tyler",
lastName: "Butler")
}
```

Simple, ha? Not so quickly. Let's run this test and see Figure 3-7.

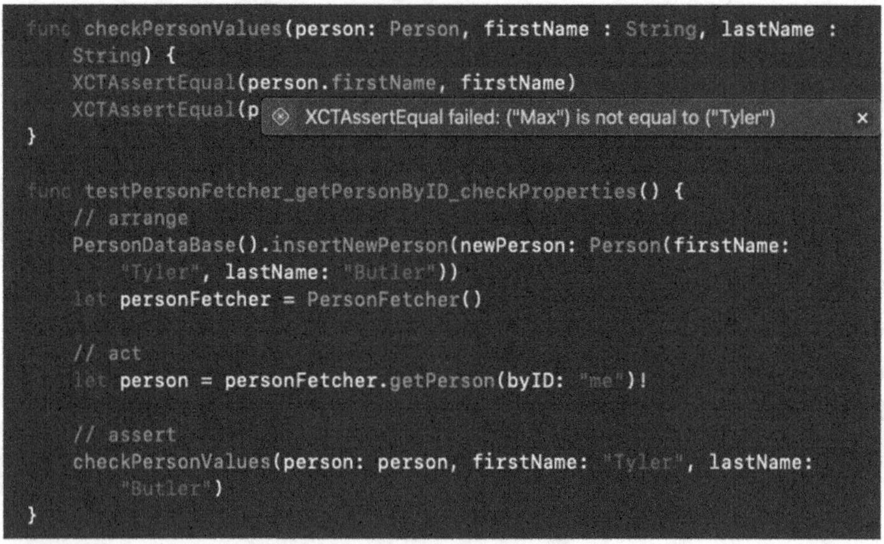

Figure 3-7. *Running test with external assertion method*

Our test failed, but this is not the issue. Do you see the problem here? From the preceding screenshot, we see the two methods – the test method and the assertion method. We also see the failure message, but instead of pointing on the test method, it points on the assertion method!

We see that we have no way of connecting the failure message to the correct test method. Also, in case of several failed test methods, we are going to have multiple failure messages in the same place, one above the other – it's a testing nightmare!

But fortunately, we have a solution. Let's look for a second on the XCTAssert function's signature:

```
func XCTAssert(_ expression: @autoclosure () throws -> Bool, _
message: @autoclosure () -> String = "", file: StaticString =
#file, line: UInt = #line)
```

As you can see, besides the expression and the message arguments, we also have two more arguments – **file** and **line**.

File (String) and Line (UInt) contain the information on where in the code XCTest shows the failure message. By default, both of them have the values of the place where we call the assertion function.

Note   *#file* and *#line* are two expressions that are part of the Swift language. You can use them not only in your tests but also in your project code. Swift also has more interesting expressions you can use in your tests and in general, like #function, #column, and more.

So, if we want to show the message on the right place, all we need to do is to pass the #line and #file expression to our final assertion method:

```
func checkPersonValues(person: Person, firstName : String,
lastName : String, line : UInt = #line, file : StaticString
= #file) {
    XCTAssertEqual(person.firstName, firstName, file: file,
    line:line)
    XCTAssertEqual(person.lastName, lastName, file: file,
    line:line)
}
```

Let me explain what I did here – our custom assertion method has two more arguments, line and file, filled with default values. The default values are the actual place where we call the function. Later then, we pass those two arguments to the assertion methods inside, overriding their default values. I can say we are kind of tricking the system into getting a clear failure message.

Now let's run our test with our improved assertion method (Figure 3-8).

```
func checkPersonValues(person: Person, firstName : String, lastName : String, line : UInt = #line,
    file : StaticString = #file) {
    XCTAssertEqual(person.firstName, firstName, file: file, line:line)
    XCTAssertEqual(person.lastName, lastName, file: file, line:line)
}

func testPersonFetcher_getPersonByID_checkProperties() {
    // arrange
    PersonDataBase().insertNewPerson(newPerson: Person(firstName: "Tyler", lastName: "Butler"))
    let personFetcher = PersonFetcher()

    // act
    let person = personFetcher.getPerson(byID: "me")!

    // assert
    checkPersonValues(person: person, firstName: "Tyler", lastName: "Butler")
}
```

> ⊘ XCTAssertEqual failed: ("Max") is not equal to ("Tyler")   ✕
>
> ⊘ XCTAssertEqual failed: ("Wood") is not equal to ("Butler")

Figure 3-8. *Custom assertion method with line and file arguments*

Great! Now our failure message displayed is in the right place – in the test method and not in the assertion method. Also, we didn't have to change anything in the test method.

To sum it up, custom assertion methods can help you maintain your testing code easier by making it more readable and less duplicated (DRY). Whenever you feel your assertion code is a little bit complex or confusing, just write your own method. It's that easy.

Write Asynchronous Operations

Take a look at the following code:

```
func testImageProcessing() {
    // arrange
    let image = UIImage(named: "3cats")!
    let manager = CatsProcessingManager()
```

```
    // act
    var cuteCats = 0
    manager.findCuteCats(image: image) { (numberOfCuteCats) in
        cuteCats = numberOfCuteCats
    }
    // assert
    XCTAssertEqual(cuteCats, 3)
}
```

In the preceding code, we want to test the method findCuteCats(), which receives an image and is supposed to find the number of cute cats shown in the picture (which is basically the total number of cats displayed since all cats are cute).

We presented an image with three cats and expected to get three as the return answer, but the test failed. At the end of the test, the cuteCats variable is still 0, and this is because **findCuteCats() is an asynchronous method**. Our intuitive fix for that is putting the assertion line inside the completion block of the function, but this makes it even worse – now, we get a false positive and our test always succeeds because the test run ends before the completion block gets executed!

We need to find a way of keeping the test method, waiting for the findCuteCats() method to finish before it asserts it.

Expect, Wait, Fulfill, and Assert

Fortunately, XCTest has an easy solution for asynchronous operations. We base this solution on three simple parts:

- **Define the Expectation** – We need to work with some kind of expectation object that can be transferred into the completion block and to help us manage the process. The definition is done using something called XCTestExpectation.

- **Mark the Expectation As Fulfill** – It's not enough for the completion block to finish; we need to tell the expectation object we created that we have all the data that we need, and we are now ready to assert.

- **Pause the Test Method Run Until We Have an Answer** – We need to halt the run of the test method before we assert; otherwise, it will just continue to the end of the method without waiting for an answer. Also, we need to define some timeout to prevent the test execution from running forever.

XCTestExpectation Pattern

Let's look at our testImageProcessing() method refactored for asynchronous testing:

```
func testImageProcessing() {
    // arrange
    let image = UIImage(named: "cats")!
    let manager = CatsProcessingManager()

    // act
    var cuteCats = 0
    // creating an expectation to get number of cats.
    let expectation = self.expectation(description:
    "Counting number of cats") //1
    manager.findCuteCats(image: image) { (numberOfCuteCats) in
        cuteCats = numberOfCuteCats

        // we've got an answer. our expectation is
        fulfilled!
        expectation.fulfill() //2
    }
```

```
// assert
// let's wait 5 seconds before asserting...
waitForExpectations(timeout: 5.0, handler: nil) //3
XCTAssertEqual(cuteCats, 3)
}
```

In the preceding code, we can see the three parts I mentioned earlier. Let's go over them:

```
let expectation = self.expectation(description: "Counting number of cats") //1
```

When we want to create an asynchronous test, we create a XCTestExpectation object. On its initialization, we pass an informative description that can help us understand what expectation was not fulfilled if our test failed.

It is possible to create multiple expectations for the same test:

```
expectation.fulfill() //2
```

When the asynchronous operation finishes its work, we call the fulfill() method of the expectation object we created previously. In most cases, it's best practice to call the fulfill() function even when the completion block failed. Don't be confused – fulfill doesn't mean our test passed; it just means we can move on to the assertion part. The terminology of "expectation is fulfilled" can be mixed with the "Expect" part of our test, so beware!

```
waitForExpectations(timeout: 5.0, handler: nil) //3
```

Before the assertion part, we call waitForExpectations() method. What this method does is to stop the test execution until all the expectations are fulfilled or the timeout was reached.

If the timeout is reached, our test fails automatically. When all the expectations are fulfilled, it's time for you to assert:

```
XCTAssertEqual(cuteCats, 3)
```

Fulfill Multiple Times for One Expectation

There are tests when we want to execute an asynchronous code several times before we can say the expectation is fulfilled, and we can move on to the assertion part. For that kind of test, XCTestExpectation has a property called **expectedFulfillmentCount**:

```
let expectation = self.expectation(description:
"executing closure code 3 times")
expectation.expectedFulfillmentCount = 3
```

A good use case for that is a music player that needs to update the progress of the song a few times. The expectation can count the number of times it gets called and then moves on to the assertion part when it reaches a specific number.

Assert When the Expectation Is Not Fulfilled

OK, I need you to stay focused on this one. There are cases when we want to make sure a code **is not** being executed. In other words, if our expectation is fulfilled, our test fails.

In this case, we can use the **isInverted** property (default is "false"):

```
let expectation = self.expectation(description: "Code
is not executed")
expectation.isInverted = true
```

A good use case for *isInverted* property is **permissions handling**. We want to make sure parts of our code are **not being** executed in a specific configuration and states.

Expect Array of Expectations, Ordered

If you have multiple expectations in a test method, you don't have to wait for them separately. Just wait at the end of the test method while passing the array of expectations:

```
wait(for: [loadFromFileExpectation, locateCuteCatsExpectation],
timeout: 2.0)
```

You can even make sure all the expectations fulfilled in a provided order!

```
wait(for: [loadFromFileExpectation, locateCuteCatsExpectation],
timeout: 2.0, enforceOrder: true)
```

XCTestExpectation Subclasses

Now that you have "wait" + "fulfill" + "assert" tools, basically, every a-sync job can be tested using XCTestExpectation. But Xcode 8.3 brought several improvements in that area in order to make those tasks much easier to build and read.

Let's look at the following code:

```
func testIfNotificationRaised() {
    let expectation = self.expectation(description:
    "Notification Raised")
    _ = NotificationCenter.default.addObserver(forName:
    NSNotification.Name("notif"), object: nil, queue: nil,
    using: { (notification) in
        expectation.fulfill()
    })

    NotificationCenter.default.post(name: NSNotification.
    Name("notif"), object: nil)
    waitForExpectations(timeout: 0.1, handler: nil)
}
```

In this code, we are trying to test if a notification was raised. We add an observer, and when we receive it, we fulfill the expectation. In the following line, we post the notification and wait 0.1 seconds for the expectation for being fulfilled.

Simple, ha? Well, the problem is that most of our tests **don't** look like this example. The observing code is usually located somewhere else, not even in our test code, and this is also true for posting the notifications in most cases:

```
func testMyScree_savingData_checkNotificationReceived () {
    // arrange
    let dataConnector = DataLayer()
    let myScreen = MyScreen()

    // act
    dataConnector.save()

    // assert
    // checking if myScreen receives a "data updated"
    notification...
}
```

In the preceding example, we have some data layers and a UI Screen. The test is to save some data and check if the screen receives a "data updated" notification.

We understand that the posting notification code is inside the data layer and the observer code is inside the UI Screen. So how do we check it?

Note   The current discussed example is not really a "unit test," but an integration test. We'll talk about Integration tests later in this book.

OK, so we can add some closure or delegate pattern to pass the event from the myScreen class to the test method, but this requires us to change our code only to make our tests easier to test. This may be true in many cases, but not in this case – no one observes this event, only the test method.

Fortunately, we have the ability to observe notification calls in our tests very easily.

Let's solve the issue we have in our test method:

```
func testMyScreen_savingData_checkNotificationRaised () {
    // arrange
    let dataConnector = DataLayer()
    let myScreen = MyScreen()
    let expectation = self.expectation(forNotification:
    NSNotification.Name("dataUpdated"), object: nil,
    handler: nil)

    // act
    dataConnector.save()

    // assert
    waitForExpectations(timeout: 0.1, handler: nil)
}
```

As you can see, we are adding **expectation(forNotification:)**. When the notification is raised, the expectation is fulfilled. Notice we are not checking if *myScreen* receives the notification. This is something you need to do some other way, for example, checking its state.

Summary

XCTest is a robust framework, and it can help you set up an excellent testing suite very easily.

Also, we've learned how to write structured test methods and how to write them as part of a test case life cycle.

But those are only the basics – in the next chapter, we will learn how to leverage our skill and write useful and maintainable unit tests.

CHAPTER 4

Writing Tests – Advanced Techniques

More than the act of testing, the act of designing tests is one of the best bug preventers known. The thinking that must be done to create a useful test can discover and eliminate bugs before they are coded – indeed, test-design thinking can discover and eliminate bugs at every stage in the creation of software, from conception to specification, to design, coding and the rest.

—Boris Beizer

Introduction

In the previous chapter, we've learned how to write basic unit tests. But in reality, we encounter more significant problems – we need to fake or mock certain parts of our code or compare values.

In this chapter, you will learn advanced techniques in unit tests, like the following:

- How to create **test doubles**, such as Mocks, Dummies, Fakes, Stubs, and Spies

- How to **avoid using test doubles** if possible

- How to **compare values** like structs and classes

- How to **compare images** and arrays

© Avi Tsadok 2020
A. Tsadok, *Pro iOS Testing*, https://doi.org/10.1007/978-1-4842-6382-2_4

- How to **avoid duplicating your testing** code when trying to run your test method multiple times with different values

- How to create test cases **dynamically**

Test Doubles (Fake, Fake, Fake)

It's true; we have unit tests that are easy to test. There are no dependencies, no network or database, and no extra work required to make our test unit to be stable and maintainable.

But with all due respect, we know the reality is different. While we are trying to isolate our functions as much as we can, they still operate in a world with other living creatures that we need to pay attention to.

Remember that in unit tests we need to focus on one area of our code at each test. Testing a specific area of the code is the reason why we need to isolate our code from the rest of the system.

Test Double is a generic term that describes objects that behave or look like the real objects our code depended on. Faking a server-layer response might be an excellent example of that. It is almost impossible to avoid the use of test doubles, especially in unit testing.

Mocks. Mocks Everywhere (?)

One of the most common mistakes developers do when dealing with test doubles is calling them "mocks." It's not that there isn't such a thing, a "mock." It's just that this term is mistakenly used when talking about test doubles.

There are several types of test doubles, other than just a "mock." Each one of them aims to solve a different part of our test isolation mission.

Dummy

A dummy is an object that does nothing. It doesn't return any value, and you never really call it. It's an object that will never be used in the test. So why do we need it? Well, there are methods that, to initialize them, you have to pass an object from a certain type. In that case, you can create a new dummy class. The dummy can be either a subclass of the original object you need to pass or a new class that conforms to the relevant protocol:

```
class ManufactureDummy : Manufacture {

}

class CarTests: XCTestCase {

    func testCarMethod(){
        let manufactureDummy = ManufactureDummy()
        let car = Car(manufacture: manufactureDummy)

        // rest of the test method
    }

}
```

Let's examine the preceding code – we want to test the class "Car" when its constructor requires one argument, "manufacture".

But this argument is not going to be used in our test, and it's only there for code design purposes. We just want to create our car object and move on. So we create dummy manufacture, which is a subclass (or a protocol based), and pass it to the car init() method.

We can say that dummies can help us initialize objects when we have to deal with a custom init() method.

Fake

Sure, we can say that every test double is a "fake." But in this case, "fake" is an object that **always returns** the same value. A good example might be a network layer to fake a network response.

Another example can be a fake login service to help you test some login logic code:

```
class LoginService {

    var isLoggedIn : Bool {
        return true
    }
}

class FakeLoginService : LoginService {
    override var isLoggedIn : Bool {
        return true
    }
}
```

The simple "FakeLoginService" always returns true in the "isLoggedIn" variable getter. You can inject this fake object in tests that require the user to be logged in when running your test.

Stub

A Stub is a test double you can use to control its return value. We can say it's a "sophisticated fake." For example, you can use a stub to fake a return or success of a service.

Look at **LoginScreenPresenter.swift**:

```
class LoginScreenPresenter {

    var loginService : LoginService
```

```
init(loginService : LoginService) {
    self.loginService = loginService
}

func doLogin(withEmail email : String, password :
String,  completion : @escaping (String)->Void) {
    loginService.doLogin(email: email, password: password)
    { (result) in
        switch result {
        case .failure:
            completion("Failed!")
        case .success:
            completion("Success")
        }
    }
}
}
```

LoginScreenPresenter has a dependency called loginService. We want to test the message output in case of a failure or success.

For the test, we create a LoginServiceStub to control the return value of *doLogin()* method:

```
class LoginServiceStub: LoginService {

    var _loginServiceResult : LoginOperationResult = .success

    init(result : LoginOperationResult) {
        _loginServiceResult = result
    }

    override func doLogin(email: String, password: String,
    completion: (LoginOperationResult) -> Void) {
        completion(_loginServiceResult)
    }
}
```

LoginServiceStub is a subclass of the original LoginService (remember, OOP is not the only way of creating stubs; you can also use Protocol-Oriented).

We create a new initializer for the stub to set the fake login result and override the doLogin() method to return that fake value.

Now let's see how to use this stub in a test:

```
func testLoginPresenter_whenFailure_expectFailureMessage()
{
        //arrange
        let loginServiceStub = LoginServiceStub(result: .failure)
        let presenter = LoginScreenPresenter(loginService:
        loginServiceStub)
        let expectation = self.expectation(description: "Check
        Login Flow Message")

        // act
        var message = ""
        presenter.doLogin(withEmail: "avi@emailServer.com",
        password: "123456") { (resultMessage) in
            message = resultMessage
            expectation.fulfill()
        }

        self.waitForExpectations(timeout: 0.1, handler: nil)

        // assert
        XCTAssertEqual(message, "Failed!")
    }
```

Passing the loginServiceStub as an argument to the LoginPresenter sure makes writing this test easy for us, ha? Notice we can easily create another test with the same stub while passing a different return value.

Spy

Spy is the opposite of stub. We use the stub to configure a dependency of the object we are testing. In Spy, we want to inspect the side effect of our tested code.

Spy doesn't return anything; it's only there to record our calls, and we can use that information later in our assertion part – this is why it is called a "Spy."

The way a spy works is straightforward. Let's say we want to test one of the presenter methods, and we know this method calls some methods in the view. All we need to do is to create a spy, meaning some object that **conforms** to the same protocol of the view and records specific calls.

Look at Figure 4-1.

Figure 4-1. *Spy vs. Stub*

And now the code version:

```
class LoginViewSpy : LoginViewProtocol {

    var messageReceived = ""

    func showMessage(message : String) {
        messageReceived = message
    }
}
    func testLoginPresenter_whenTappedOnLoginButtonAndNoNetork_
    showError() {
        // arrange
        let loginPresenter = LoginPresenter()
```

```
        let viewSpy = LoginViewSpy()
        loginPresenter.view = viewSpy

        // act
        loginPresenter.onLoginButtonTapped()

        // assert
        let messageReceived = viewSpy.messageReceived
        XCTAssertEqual(messageReceived, "Error. Please check
        your network")
    }
```

In the preceding code, we have our LoginPresenter that needs to update its view.

Usually, its View is some kind of a UIViewController that conforms to LoginViewProtocol, but in this case, we created a spy. Just a regular class that conforms to the same protocol and the presenter doesn't know he updates the Spy and not the real view controller. This Spy saves the message it receives in a variable, and later the method asserts and verifies the received message.

Spies are a widespread test double, and the inspection can go further – you can inspect the order of the calls or even how many calls were made.

Mock

I mentioned earlier that from many developer's perspective, all test doubles are mocks, and this a common mistake. Up until now, we discussed Dummy, Fake, Stub, and Spy.

So, what is a Mock? Well, a mock is a sophisticated and more independent spy. Mock also records method call information. But unlike a spy, it knows what to expect and does the verification itself.

In real mocks (it's weird to name mocks "real"), we define the expectations on the setup, and the mocks verify them on the assertion part.

The mock object usually has a function "verify()" to make sure it meets the expectations.

Let's rewrite our test with mock instead of a spy:

```
class LoginViewMock : LoginViewProtocol {

    var expectedMessage = ""
    private var messageReceived = ""

    func showMessage(message : String) {
        messageReceived = message
    }

    func verify()->Bool {
        return messageReceived == expectedMessage
    }
}
    func testLoginPresenter_whenTappedOnLoginButtonAndNoNetork_
    showError() {
        // arrange
        let loginPresenter = LoginPresenter()
        let viewMock = LoginViewMock()
        loginPresenter.view = viewMock

        // setup expectations
        viewMock.expectedMessage = "Error. Please check your
        network"

        // act
        loginPresenter.onLoginButtonTapped()

        // assert
        XCTAssertTrue(viewMock.verify())
    }
```

In the rewritten test method, we are now using a mock instead of a spy. We define the expected message, and in the assert part, we are checking the verify() method. The comparison between the expected message and the received message is done **inside the mock** and not in the test method.

While this may not sound like a big deal, in fact, it is, especially in unit testing.

First, remember we talked about the arrange part – we said we need to set up the state of the test in that part. But when dealing with mocks, we also need to set up its expectations.

Second, in stubs, we do **state verifications**, meaning we are checking to see if the stub made the right calls to the mock. But in mocks, we do **behavior verification**. In this case, we don't care about the actual calls made to the mock, but instead, we want to know that the mock object responded right to our "act" part of the test.

Complete vs. Partial Mocking

We have two ways of mocking objects – "complete" and "partial." In some of the examples I presented, we create the test double by conforming to a protocol. In other cases, we subclass the original type and override some of its methods. So, we see there is a difference in the way we choose how to create our test doubles.

Partial Mocking is when we create a test double while modifying and changing the original type (class or struct). The mocking is done by subclassing and overriding the specific methods we want to change.

In **Complete Mocking**, we create our test double from scratch. This is usually done by conforming to a protocol, represented the original type.

In general, partial mocking is closer to the real code and is "less fake." I think that we need to avoid partial mocking. Using partial mocking might be OK in the short run, but in the long term, modifying the existing types may encounter problems. Working with a modified real object can lead to unexpected behavior, while these objects are being changed over time due to code evolution.

Avoid Test Doubles If Possible

OK. What? We just had a long session about how to create great test doubles to help us test our code. So how come I recommend you not to use test doubles if possible?

Well, in many cases (not all!), test doubles consider being a code smell. A code smell is an indication of a deeper problem you might have in your code – maybe some anti-pattern you are using or a wrong structure. If you heavily rely on test doubles for testing, it might be code coupling, and code coupling is not ideal for unit testing.

Coupling

When a type (class/struct) works with another type, we call it **coupling**. In general, we want to reduce coupling in our app to the minimum (zero is not realistic. After all, it's a system). Think of two objects that work together – the more they know about each other, the more chances this relationship will break in the future. Classes evolve and change, and those changes may have impacts on other related classes as well.

Types of Coupling

But what exactly do we mean when we say "coupled objects"?There are several types of coupling – **Subclass, Shared Object, Dependencies, and Side Effects**.

Subclass Coupling – When a class is inherited from another class, it depended on its superclass, and those two classes become coupled. Not only that – the entire inheritance hierarchy is coupled. But this is just logical – think how little you know what happens when you override a method in a class with five levels of inheritance. Many developers subclass when they could just use a protocol instead and reduce coupling.

Shared Objects – When different objects mutate properties on a shared object, and at the same time, they depend on it, they are coupled **through the shared objects**. Re-think whether the shared object is required to be shared. This is one of the drawbacks with the Singleton pattern – sharing an object throughout the system reduces your ability to predict how your code behaves as a system.

Second, you need to think about restrictions for changing the shared object state – what objects allow to change its state and when. The fewer objects can change the state, the smaller the coupling is.

Dependencies – If your class relies on another class without a chance to change it, you've got a tight coupling here. There are many ways to decouple such a thing – from injecting new dependencies, delegate patterns, protocol-based dependency, or even using a closure.

Side Effects – Always examine your code for side effects. If you have a function that modifies other object's properties or changes persistent data, these are side effects. Try to reduce side effects to a minimum. Follow the "Single-Responsibility Principle" to isolate these side effects to one place and by that loosen the coupling of your objects.

How to Decouple Existing Code?

Decoupling an existing code doesn't have to be a big refactor task. Sometimes small changes are enough to reduce the coupling level in your project.

First, let's understand what coupling levels are.

Coupling Severity Levels

We have four levels of severity:

Tightly Coupled – A class holds a dependency that cannot be replaced at all, not even with the same class. "Tightly coupled" usually happens when the dependency is a constant ("let") and cannot be set.

Coupled – In "coupled," the dependency relies on a particular class, meaning we can change the dependency with an object from the same class or one of its subclasses (unless it's marked as "final"). Although it still considered a coupled relationship, it's much better than tightly coupled. Usually, this can be done by making the dependency a public variable or adding a constructor to set the dependency upon initializing.

Loosely Coupled – In loosely coupled, the class is not dependent on a specific class but rather a protocol. Loosely coupled expands the spectrum of possibilities even further by letting you connect objects without constraining them to their implementation. Loosely coupled is the level when you can easily create mocks/stubs and connect them during testing. You can also combine different objects with different implementation in runtime.

Decoupled – In the "decoupled" level, the relationship between objects is not based on a class type or even a protocol. It doesn't mean there are no dependencies at all – we do have dependencies. But they can communicate through closure or a notification. When this is done, not only can you reuse your classes across your project; chances are you can also do it between other projects (sometimes with minor changes).

Make Changes to Your Code

Let's see how we can change our code to improve our coupling levels.

Here we have our LoginPresenter class:

```
class LoginPresenter {

    let networkClient = NetworkClient()

}
```

We see this class has a dependency named "networkClient". Because it's a "let" dependency, this means we cannot change it at all. Therefore, it's a **Tightly Coupled** level. If we want to improve our coupling level, we just need to make a small modification – change "let" to "var":

```
class LoginPresenter {

    var networkClient = NetworkClient()

}
```

Great! Now we can change the networkClient variable to a different object, as long as it's from the same class (NetworkClient) or one of its subclasses.

Now, we are no longer in **Tightly Coupled**, and we upgraded the coupling level to **Coupled**. But we don't have to stop here – we can add one more thing to improve it:

```
class LoginPresenter {

    var networkClient : NetworkClientProtocol = NetworkClient()

}
```

Now our variable is no longer from the type "NetworkClient". In fact, the networkClient variable can hold any object that conforms to NetworkClientProtocol. This lets us connect other objects with different implementation and even mocks and stubs.

The use of a protocol leverages our coupling level to **Loosely Coupled**.

As mentioned before, we can skip the three steps and go straight to **Decoupling** level, where we can use a closure or a notification.

In this way, the class that calls the closure or the notification doesn't care about the type or the interface of the dependency. In most cases, it doesn't even care that there is a dependency:

```
typealias doLoginClosure = ()->Void

class LoginPresenter {

    var doLoginClosure : doLoginClosure?
```

```
func onLoginButtonTapped() {
    doLoginClosure?()
}
}
```

The latest example is simple, but it makes the term "Decoupled" much clearer.

Decoupled objects reduce the number of mocking you need to do in your tests. When any object or piece of code can be a dependency, even your testing method can implement the desired behavior for your test.

There Are More Ways to Reduce Coupling

Another way to reduce coupling is how you write your functions. The same principles we follow on objects can be implemented in functions as well. For example, Pure Functions (which we already discussed) are an excellent example of decoupling pieces of code from each other.

The same goes for function size – when you have a function that handles several tasks, you are **coupling responsibilities together**.

Take a look at the following code:

```
class myScreenPresenter {

    var view : myScreenViewProtocol?

    func onTappedSave(fileURL : URL) {
        NetworkClient.shared.fetchCities {[weak self] (data) in
            try! data?.write(to: fileURL)
            NotificationCenter.default.post(name: NSNotification.
            Name(rawValue: "DataSavedNotification"), object: nil)
            self?.view?.dismiss()
        }
    }
}
```

The method onTappedSave() has too many responsibilities – it goes to the network, saves the returned value, posts a notification, and also asks the view to dismiss itself. We already know that we need to write single-responsibility functions, but this is part of the reason why – we are chaining too many tasks together. Not only it's a bad practice – but it also makes us fake the network client anytime we want to test something not related to fetching the requests (like saving or processing the data).

Creating small functions also helps us reduce the use of test doubles by creating short pieces of code that, in many cases, don't need mocks.

Comparing

The assertion part is not always that simple. Comparing Int, Strings, and Boolean values is straightforward. But what about comparing your classes? And colors? Arrays?

In some cases, you need to add changes to your code to make your tests easier on the assertion part.

The Problem with Comparing

Let's say we have a "Person" class:

```
class Person {
    var personID : String
    var firstName : String
    var lastName : String

    init(personID : String, firstName : String, lastName :
    String) {
        self.personID   = personID
```

```
        self.firstName  = firstName
        self.lastName   = lastName
    }
}
```

In our tests, we want to compare two "Persons" to see if they are equal. We can do something like this:

```
XCTAssertEqual(person1.personID,person2.personID)
XCTAssertEqual(person1.firstName,person2.firstName)
XCTAssertEqual(person1.lastName,person2.lastName)
```

Sure, it works, but admit it doesn't look like an elegant assertion part. Also, writing a custom assertion method as we've learned has a code smell that something is wrong here – we are trying to compare two objects from the same class. It should be naturally possible.

We can also try this one:

```
XCTAssertEqual(person1, person2)
```

But this doesn't even compile – we get a complication error:

```
Global function 'XCTAssertEqual(_:_:_:file:line:)' requires
that 'Person' conform to 'Equatable'
```

The error message states that "Person" needs to conform to the "Equatable" protocol. What does it mean?

Equatable Protocol

Primitive values (Int, String, Boolean) are easy to compare and assert, but classes and structs require extra work.

To compare different objects or structs, we need to extend those types and implement the **Equatable** protocol.

Let's take the example of a "Person" class:

```
extension Person : Equatable {

    static func ==(lhs: Person, rhs : Person)->Bool {
        return lhs.personID == rhs.personID
    }

}
```

In this code snippet, we make the comparison of Person using the "personID" property, but you can also extend it to first and last name if you want.

Now, the XCTAssertEqual(person1, person2) is working correctly, and you can use it in your tests just like primitive values.

Comparable Protocol

Sometimes Equatable is not useful enough to create easy tests, and we need something more elaborate. This is where the Comparable protocol gets in.

If Equatable lets us define equality and inequality, Comparable protocol, which is built on top of Equatable, lets you compare between objects and identify which is "bigger" or "smaller." "Comparable" is helpful with ordering tasks, but it's also useful for testing.

Let's take our "Person" class and add it an "age" property:

```
class Person {
    var personID : String
    var firstName : String
    var lastName : String
    var age : Int
```

```
init(personID : String, firstName : String, lastName :
String, age : Int) {
    self.personID   =   personID
    self.firstName  =   firstName
    self.lastName   =   lastName
    self.age        =   age
    }
}
```

Now we want to compare it by its **age** property. Using the "<" and ">" operators doesn't work because we need to define exactly how to compare two persons.

Let's extend "Person" using Comparable protocol:

```
extension Person : Comparable {
    static func < (lhs : Person, rhs: Person) -> Bool {
        return lhs.age < rhs.age
    }
}
```

Now it's perfectly fine to use the compared "Person" by size:

```
XCTAssertGreaterThan(person1, person2)
```

You probably noticed something unique here. We know we can use "<", ">", "<=", and ">=" operators when comparing objects. In Comparable protocol, implementing only the "<" function does the job for the rest of the operators. By the way, is the "<" function? It should also be tested, of course.

Compare UIImages

If you want to test a method that generates images, you probably want to verify that the generated image is the correct one. Unfortunately, comparing UIImages just by using the "==" operator doesn't work.

Lucky for us, we have simple tools to fix that.

The trick is to convert those images to Data and compare the two data objects. Using the image data comparison makes it possible to conform to the Equatable protocol we discussed earlier:

```
func ==(lhs: UIImage, rhs: UIImage) -> Bool {
    if let lhsData = lhs.pngData(), let rhsData = rhs.pngData() {
        return lhsData == rhsData
    }
    return false
}
```

And then:

```
XCTAssertEqual(image1, image2)
```

Comparing UIImage may not sound like a common task in testing, but when you have a use case for that, this extension can save you a lot of time.

Compare Arrays

Comparing Arrays can be a little bit tricky since we have several issues we need to address here:

- We need to make sure the items in the array **can be compared**. If the array doesn't contain primitive values (Int, String, Boolean) but references or structs, we need to make sure they are all compliant with Comparable or Equatable protocols, as discussed earlier.

- We need to decide if we care about **the order of the elements**. Sometimes we just want to check if both arrays contain the same elements regardless of their order.

- Another thing is **duplicate elements** – unlike *Set*,
  Arrays can contain duplicate items. Does a duplicate
  item cause our test to fail, or can we ignore it?

These are questions you need to ask yourself when you want to assert arrays.

Comparison Is Critical in Testing

Comparison is an essential part of writing code, but in testing, it's even more critical. Comparing objects and values is one of the most common tasks we do in the assertion part of the test, and the most dangerous thing that can happen to us is **False Negative**, due to inadequate implementation of Equatable protocol.

Also, using Equatable and Comparison protocols can simplify your testing techniques, so you should learn them deeply.

Parameterized Unit Tests

Let's say we are building a calendar application, and we write a great function that takes a list of calendar events and generate layout information to help us display them on the screen.

The function signature looks something like this:

```
class CalendarLayoutGenerator {

    func generateLayout(events : [Event])->LayoutStructure {
        // This is where the generated code takes apart.
    }
}
```

Writing a test method for the "generateLayout()" function seems straightforward. We need to create an array of *Event* objects, an expected *LayoutStructure*, run the test method, and compare between them. It's not a complicated work for such an important test:

```
func testGenerateLayout() {
        var events = [Event]()
        events.append(Event(startTime: generateDateFromString
        (str: "04/27/2020 10:00"), endTime:
        generateDateFromString(str : "04/27/2020 11:00")))
        events.append(Event(startTime: generateDateFromString
        (str: "04/27/2020 10:30"), endTime:
        generateDateFromString(str : "04/27/2020 11:20")))
        events.append(Event(startTime: generateDateFromString
        (str: "04/28/2020 12:30"), endTime:
        generateDateFromString(str : "04/28/2020 14:20")))

        var expectedStructure = LayoutStructure()
        // modify expectedStructure with the expected results

        // act
        let actualStructure = CalendarLayoutGenerator().
        generateLayout(events: events)

        // assert
        XCTAssertEqual(actualStructure, expectedStructure)
    }
```

The preceding testing method refers to only one use case; however, we have many layout variations we want to verify.

So, we can duplicate our testing method and just change/add/remove the relevant values.

Duplicating a method can be a decent solution for 2–3 cases, but what if we want to run the same test with 10–15 data variations?

Duplicating our testing method so many times may work on the first day, but over time, it can cause our tests to break.

Any small change to the generateLayout() method signature forces us to "find and replace" all the test methods in the class.

Any improvement to the assertion part makes us refactor all the test methods.

Any small change in our testing mechanism or our execution code might require us to work hard and modify the long list of tests we created.

What we need to do to make our testing code more maintainable is to find a way of running multiple test cases, where the **only difference between them is the data**. One option is to create an abstracting layer above our test methods.

Create Abstract Method for Testing

The trick is straightforward. We create a method (called "runTest" for that matter) in this example that does all the dirty work – all the setup, connections, and assertion, and all the stuff you don't want to repeat yourself every test and has nothing to do with the actual data being tested.

For your actual test cases, you create an explicit test method for each one of them. These test methods do not assert but, instead, call our "dirty" function while passing the relevant data.

Here is an example:

```
func runTest(withData events : [Event], expectedLayout :
LayoutStructure, file : StaticString = #file, line : UInt =
#line) {
        // act
        let actualStructure = CalendarLayoutGenerator().
        generateLayout(events: events)
```

```swift
        // assert
        XCTAssertEqual(actualStructure, expectedLayout, file :
        file, line : line)
    }

    func testGenerateLayout_abstractMethod1() {
        var events = [Event]()
        events.append(Event(startTime: generateDateFromString
        (str: "04/27/2020 10:00"), endTime:
        generateDateFromString(str : "04/27/2020 11:00")))
        events.append(Event(startTime: generateDateFromString
        (str: "04/27/2020 10:30"), endTime:
        generateDateFromString(str : "04/27/2020 11:20")))
        events.append(Event(startTime: generateDateFromString
        (str: "04/28/2020 12:30"), endTime:
        generateDateFromString(str : "04/28/2020 12:30")))

        let expectedLayout = LayoutStructure()

        runTest(withData: events, expectedLayout:
        LayoutStructure())
    }

    func testGenerateLayout_abstractMethod2() {
        var events = [Event]()
        events.append(Event(startTime: generateDateFromString
        (str: "04/28/2020 10:00"), endTime:
        generateDateFromString(str : "04/28/2020 11:00")))
        events.append(Event(startTime: generateDateFromString
        (str: "04/28/2020 10:30"), endTime:
        generateDateFromString(str : "04/29/2020 11:20")))
```

```
events.append(Event(startTime: generateDateFromString
(str: "04/29/2020 12:30"), endTime:
generateDateFromString(str : "04/30/2020 12:30")))

let expectedLayout = LayoutStructure()

runTest(withData: events, expectedLayout:
LayoutStructure())
    }
```

In the preceding code example, the "runTest()" method is simple, to demonstrate how to implement this pattern in more complicated test methods.

Also, notice the test method receives the *file* and *line* parameters to show the precise location where the test fails.

Loading Test Cases from a File

Another option we can do to do parameterized unit tests is to load the test cases **from a file**.

Instead of creating a test method manually for each use case, we can create a JSON file with an array of all test cases, load, and iterate the array.

Let's take a look at a potentially JSON file, containing several test cases:

```
{
    "test":[
        {
            "name":"test1",
            "events":[
                {
                    "startDate":"04/27/2020 10:00",
                    "endDate":"04/27/2020 11:00"
                },
```

```
        {
            "startDate":"04/27/2020 10:30",
            "endDate":"04/27/2020 11:20"
        },
        {
            "startDate":"04/28/2020 12:30",
            "endDate":"04/28/2020 12:30"
        }
    ],
    "expectedStructure":"--=--"
},
{
    "name":"test2",
    "events":[
        {
            "startDate":"04/27/2020 10:30",
            "endDate":"04/27/2020 11:30"
        },
        {
            "startDate":"04/27/2020 10:45",
            "endDate":"04/27/2020 11:50"
        },
        {
            "startDate":"04/28/2020 12:20",
            "endDate":"04/28/2020 15:30"
        }
    ],
    "expectedStructure":"--=--"
}
]
}
```

The goal of the "name" property for each test case is to point at a specific test case if a failure occurs. Loading test cases from a file has many advantages:

- It's **effortless to add** more test cases. You can do that with any editor or external script.

- It's also **easy to validate** those tests. Since it's a JSON file, your parsing code requires a specific structure to run the tests. Think about the previous example of creating more and more methods. What are the odds of having a mistake with that process?

- **Anybody can write those tests.** You don't have to know Swift or even coding to add more test cases. Heck, you don't also have to know JSON – it's possible to write them in Excel or some other tool and later on generate a JSON file. Working with JSON is extremely practical when you want your QA team to be a part of test writing.

- The opportunity to save your tests in a **readable file** can make your life easier when trying to understand what exactly you are testing and what scenarios you're covering.

- It's excellent for **cross-platform testing**. Many tools help you write cross-platform code. But if you insist on writing native code on each platform, sharing tests is a great way to make sure the implementations are on the same standards.

One thing to notice when loading data from a JSON file is that you cannot use the main bundle for that. The main bundle is only for execution code, not frameworks and test code.

You should do something like this:

```
Bundle(for: type(of: self)).path(forResource: "tests", ofType:
"json")
```

Invoke Tests Dynamically

Loading tests from a file is a great way to create many unit tests in a readable and accessible format. But we have a problem here; when we want to read our test report at the end of the run, we're going to see only one test – the test method that loads the file and loops all the cases.

Fortunately, XCTest has a neat feature that lets you invoke tests dynamically and add them to the test run on runtime.

The XCTestRun Environment

Before we move on with loading tests dynamically, we need to understand the test runtime environment. Take a look at Figure 4-2.

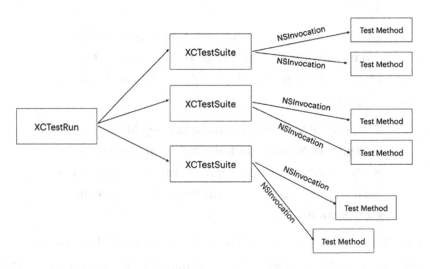

Figure 4-2. *XCTestRun environment*

We previously discussed the testing runtime, but in fact, running tests is a complicated task needed to be managed. XCTest framework uses several tools to accomplish that.

The first one is **XCTestRun**. XCTestRun is an instance created when you start your test. It contains useful information, such as the start date of the test run, duration, failure count, and more. Also, XCTestRun represented in a file contains the list of tests and assets.

In every test run, we also have **XCTestSuite**. XCTestSuite is created for every XCTestCase, and it groups the tests according to the corresponding XCTestCase it belongs to.

Think of XCTestCase as planning and XCTestSuite as the execution.

Also, remember, XCTestCase instance is created for every test method, as we discussed before.

Every XCTestSuite has a list of **NSInvocations** which forwards the message to the actual test methods that need to run.

XCTestSuite is created automatically on runtime and managed by XCTestRun.

So, if we want to invoke test methods on runtime, we need to find a way to invoke more tests in the already created XCTestSuite.

If right now you are confused with the "XCT**" classes mentioned, that's perfectly normal. Let's try to understand it with some code examples.

First Step – Override defaultTestSuite() Variable

Each XCTestCase has a class variable called *defaultTestSuite()*:

```
class var defaultTestSuite : XCTestSuite { get }
```

XCTestRun uses this variable to get the corresponding test suite for the current XCTestCase and to run all tests included. What we need to do is to **override this variable** and return our own XCTestSuite.

Creating XCTestSuite Object

To create a relevant test suite which is based on the current XCTestCase, we need to initialize it with the name of the current XCTestCase subclass:

```
let testSuite = XCTestSuite(name: NSStringFromClass(self))
```

Passing the class name of the XCTestCase creates a test suite with all the tests derived from the test case itself.

Create and Add New Test Cases On the Fly

Now that we have a test suite, we can add new test cases and run them. But, some of you might notice a problem here – test methods cannot have any parameters, and in our case, we need to create a test case with different data each time.

If you recall from previous chapters, XCTestRun creates an XCTestCase instance **for every test method** that it runs.

For example, if we test a case with four test methods, we are going to have four XCTestCase instances, one for each test method.

This mechanism also applies here. For every test method, we need to

- Create a new XCTestCase instance

- Initialize it with the test method invocation (to connect it to the right method)

- Customize it with data using custom properties

- Add it to the test suite

While it might sound difficult to understand, it's quite simple. Let's see the full code in action:

```
class FullNamesGeneratorTests: XCTestCase {

var names = [String]()
var expectedFullName = ""
```

```swift
override class var defaultTestSuite: XCTestSuite {
    get {
        let testSuite = XCTestSuite(name:
        NSStringFromClass(self))

        addNewTest(withNames: ["Avi", "Tsadok"],
        expectedResult: "Avi Tsadok", testSuite: testSuite)
        addNewTest(withNames: ["Bill", "Gates"],
        expectedResult: "Bill Gates", testSuite: testSuite)
        addNewTest(withNames: ["Steve", "Jobs"],
        expectedResult: "Steve Ballmer", testSuite:
        testSuite)

        return testSuite
    }
}

class func addNewTest(withNames names : [String],
expectedResult : String, testSuite : XCTestSuite) {
    for invocation in self.testInvocations {

        let newTestCase = FullNamesGeneratorTests(invocati
        on: invocation)
        newTestCase.names = names
        newTestCase.expectedFullName = expectedResult

        testSuite.addTest(newTestCase)
    }
}

func testFullNameGenerator() {
    var fullName = ""
    for name in names {
        fullName += name
```

```
    if name != names.last! {
        fullName += " "
    }
}

XCTAssertEqual(fullName, expectedFullName)
}

}
```

What do we have here? Let's try to understand it together.

The FullNamesGeneratorTests class has two methods, two properties, and one class-level property. The goal of this class is to test a piece of code that takes an array of names and produces a full name string:

- **"names" Property** – This variable contains our input for the test method.

- **"expectedFullName" Property** – This is our expected result from the test method.

- **testFullNameGenerator()** – This is the actual test method of the class. It takes the "names" property, trying to build a string out of it, and compares it to the "expectedFullName" property.

- **"addNewTest" Class Method** – This method loops all the class invocation (there is one invocation for each test method), creates a new test case, sets its "names" and "expectedFullName" properties, and adds it to the received test suite.

- **Class Variable defaultTestSuite** – After we create a new test suite, we expand its test list (using "addNew-Test" function) and return the modified suite.

What's excellent with invoking new test cases on the run is that it affects our test report and makes it more reliable and accurate.

Look at our test report now (Figure 4-3).

Figure 4-3. *Test report with three new test cases*

Did you see it? testFullNameGenerator function ran three times and failed on the third run.

Parameterized tests are a great way to dynamically add more and more tests without writing new test methods or duplicating your code. It's an excellent example of how to treat your testing code like a "real code," with a dynamic approach and DRY principle.

Summary

In this chapter, we covered advanced techniques in unit testing, and this should give you the tools to write your own maintainable and effective unit tests quickly.

While unit testing is significant and essential, you should remember we also need to test our app as an integrated system. This is what "Integration Tests" are for – to allow you to test your app closer to the user.

Summary

CHAPTER 5

Integration Tests

Debugging is twice as hard as writing the code in the first place. Therefore, if you write the code as cleverly as possible, you are, by definition, not smart enough to debug it.

—Brian W. Kernighan

Introduction

In the previous chapters, we learned how to test a specific unit. We discussed how to isolate it from the rest of the app and focus on its specific implementation.

However, our project is not just a bunch of functions needed to be tested. It's a whole system designed to work together.

In this chapter, you will learn

- Why it's essential to add Integration tests to your project

- What is the cost of Integration tests vs. unit tests

- How to define the scope of our tests

- How to write a simple integration test

- How to write incremental integration tests

- What is "Bottom-Up" and "Top-Down" testing

- How to write Client-Server tests, including Black Box and White Box

© Avi Tsadok 2020
A. Tsadok, *Pro iOS Testing*, https://doi.org/10.1007/978-1-4842-6382-2_5

The Idea Behind Integration Tests

The roots for the idea of integration tests were planted years ago, where developer's teams tried to come up with a big, complicated system. The problem was that each team had its mission – to develop a module that needed to be integrated later on into a bigger module. While each team took care of writing a unit test to make sure its code performs as expected, the big challenge was to combine all the modules.

Think of this challenge as a sports team with very talented players. It's not enough for the players to be in good shape – they also need to work together as a team, especially to improve their communication with each other.

What Exactly Are Integration Tests

Most of the features we create are built upon **modules** or **layers**. An example of such a layer is the UI layer represented by UIViewController. A presenter/ViewModel can be another layer. Interactor, a business logic, a calendar connector, and a network layer are additional examples of layers that we have in our app.

In fact, it's not unusual to find an app with five, six, or even seven layers.

The recommended workflow is first to test each layer of its own and then test how all units work together (see Figure 5-1).

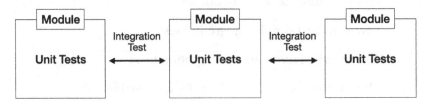

Figure 5-1. *Integration Tests – Unit Test each layer and then the communication between them*

Notice that an integration test can be between two modules or more or the whole system.

Integration Tests vs. Unit Tests

The first confusion developers have with integration tests is with the creation of such a test. If you recall, we have only two ways to create a test in XCTest – UI and Unit Tests. Integration Tests fall under Unit Tests in this case.

Another confusion is what exactly considered to be **an integration**. For instance, if you test a function that relies on another logic function, is that an integration? And let's say that this function uses some helper class in your project, is that integration as well? After all, two classes talk to each other – sounds like integration to me.

Well, not every communication between classes and functions is considered being an "integration" in our case.

In iOS Integration Tests, it is common to test integration between layers of our architecture, which means testing the layers according to the data flow and not just the use of external functions or classes.

Also, in Unit Tests, we have **heavy use of test doubles**. It's not that integration tests don't include test doubles – they are, but much less and mostly on the edges (we'll cover that later).

Define the Scope

I previously mentioned that integration tests refer to data flows between layers. Remember that some of those layers are harder to test. For example, the **Network Layer** is responsible for the communication with our server. This requires not only network connections and a live server, but sometimes tokens and other authentication data. Another example of a hard-to-test layer might be on the other side of our system – the **UI layer**. In this layer, we often required to load classes from XIB files or Storyboards.

In general, when dealing with Integration Tests, we need to define our **testing scope**. On the one hand, it's ideal for testing the whole system (edge to edge), from UI layer all the way down to the server. On the other hand, tests like that are harder to write and maintain and would run slower.

Take a look of schematic feature architecture (Figure 5-2).

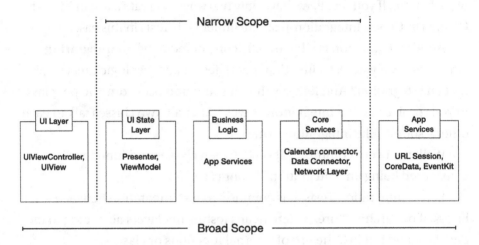

Figure 5-2. *Integration Tests scope*

Figure 5-2 displays a classic screen architecture – from the UI Layer down to the iOS SDK frameworks. You can see we can do extensive testing, meaning do some action on the UI Layer and examine the effect on the other edge (e.g., Core Data), or do a narrow test – test some of the layers and use test doubles for the rest of the system.

Filling the Gap

Although Narrow Integration tests are very cost-effective, some may argue they don't test the system as a whole. This may be true, but we can overcome it. We can easily divide our integration tests into different suites – one suite can test several layers (from the UI to the app core services), and another suite can focus on Client-Server integration tests.

Separating our integration tests to different test classes or bundles can help us run them at different frequencies. The question is "is it worth all that trouble?"

It's like Unit Tests vs. Integration Tests Ratio

If you remember from the first chapter, we talked about the testing pyramid and that we should come up with a reasonable mix between the different test suites.

One of the considerations we have is the ratio between effectiveness and cost. Take a look at Figure 5-3.

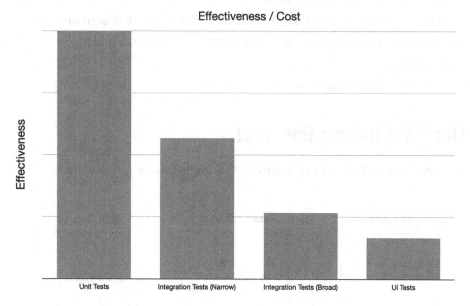

Figure 5-3. *The effectiveness of the different types of testing*

The preceding figure is a rough estimate regarding the ratio between cost and effectiveness. As you can see, Narrow Integration Tests are much more useful than Broad Integration Tests, just like the difference between Unit Tests and Integration Tests in general.

Too many integration tests can make you spend much time maintaining them from breaking up, more time than Unit Tests. On the other hand, testing the critical flows gives you more confidence in your app and your code.

Writing Integration Tests

Technically wise, writing integration tests is much like writing unit tests. Unit Test and UI Test are the technical names of the templates, not their methodological names. Integration Tests fall **under Unit Tests** and use the same assertion and function structure.

However, Integration Tests require more preliminary design process and broader knowledge and awareness of the feature and screen architecture.

Let's try to write our first Integration Test.

Our First Integration Test

We have a basic To-Do App (Figure 5-4) with just three components.

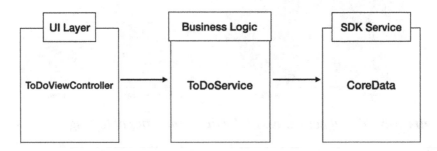

Figure 5-4. *A basic To-Do App with three layers*

Our To-Do app is built with three layers – the UI Layer (the screen itself), basic business logic, and a core data persistent store, which is responsible for handling the state of the to-do items.

The test case we want to write is when the user marks an item as "checked"; the item is expected to be also marked as "checked" in our Core Data store. Obviously, this is an Integration Test, verifying that our three layers work together seamlessly.

Let's see how our layers supposed to work together:

- The user presses the "mark" button on the view controller.

- The Business Logic receives the tap and receives the corresponding item.

- The Business Logic updates the item state property to "checked".

- The Data Connector updates the data in our CoreData persistent store.

Now let's take a look at our test method:

```swift
func testMarkItemAsChecked_verifySavedInStore() {
    // arrange
    let viewController = ToDoListItemsViewController(nibNa
    me: "ToDoListItemsViewController", bundle: nil)
    viewController.loadViewIfNeeded()
    let itemID = UUID().uuidString
    _ = CoreDataConnector.shared.insertNewItem(title: "my
    Item", id: itemID)
    viewController.itemID = itemID

    // act
    viewController.markItemAsCheckedButtonTapped()

    // assert
    let item = CoreDataConnector.shared.getItem(byID: itemID)!
    XCTAssertTrue(item.checked)
}
```

First, just like Unit Tests, we also have our AAA pattern – Arrange-Act-Assert.

In the "Arrange" section, we initialized our UI Layer and, in our case, a UIViewController.

Notice for an unusual call we did there:

```
viewController.loadViewIfNeeded()
```

The method "loadViewIfNeeded()" forces the view to load even if we didn't add it to the screen. This is extremely useful in testing when dealing with UI elements is not trivial.

After initializing the UI Layer, we prepare our database and insert a new item to our core data store.

The "**Act**" part is pretty straightforward – since we already loaded the view in the arrange part, all our IBOutlets and IBActions are connected. We can simulate pressing on the mark button by just calling its IBAction.

In the **Assert** part, we go straight to the DataConnector and fetch the relevant CoreData object and assert its "checked" value.

As you can you, we tested how three layers integrate, without the need of any test doubles.

But, there are a couple of things that we need to pay attention to, especially in Integration Tests:

– **Always clean after your test**. Integration tests change states, write files, and modify databases. This can influence the results not only for the next test you run but also for tests that are running in parallel. Take into consideration that you already have some data saved on your device/simulator, and your app is not "clean" when you start your test.

– As a result of what is said, you need to **run your integration tests in isolation** from other tests. Remember, your tests share the same resources. It is better different persistent store files or other UserDefaults settings for each test.

- You have to assume your **app state is unpredictable** when you start your test. If you manage some authentication state such as "logged in" and it has an impact on your tests, reset it before you start (you can use the setup() method).

Running in Parallel

As you can see, running in parallel can cause us a headache when dealing with shared resources. However, there are ways to overcome that.

For instance, using an In-Memory Core Data store can help you separate it from other tests. Launching your test with different SQLite file names can also be useful.

Fault Point in Integration Tests

One of the challenges we have when writing Integration Tests is to identify our fault point when the test fails.

Unlike Unit Tests, in Integration Tests, our data flow goes through several layers, when each one of them can be the cause of our issue. To be specific, the source of the problem might not be the layer, but the **integration between two layers**. Fortunately, some techniques can help us get on the problem and locate precisely where it fails.

A Bigger System to Test

Identifying the fault point may not seem like a big issue when dealing with a three-layer architecture. But there are features and architectures with five to six layers that are more difficult to integrate and debug.

Let's take a look at such a system (Figure 5-5).

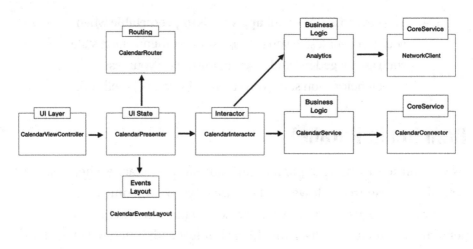

Figure 5-5. *A complex feature with five layers*

Figure 5-5 describes a design for a feature with five layers, starting from the UI and ending with core services that connect to the device calendar and network.

How do we write an efficient integration test for such an architecture in a way that can help us track issues? One approach can be an **incremental integration test**.

Incremental Integration Test

We know that testing integration between several layers can be an issue, but testing integration between two layers is much more straightforward. In Incremental testing, we take our architecture and start with the first two layers. At each step, we add one more layer to our test and recheck it until we add all of our layers.

In this way, we are re-testing our integration in each step, which makes it easier for us to locate the problem.

But how exactly can we test one layer at a time? After all, we are not dealing with Lego cubes.

Well, there are mainly two ways of implementing an Incremental Integration Test – **Bottom-Up** and **Top-Down**.

Bottom-Up

If the UI layer is considered to be the "Top" layer of our architecture, the core services layer is the "Bottom" one. When talking about "top" and "bottom," we usually refer to layers that are closer to the user level as "Top" and layers that are closer to the system level as "Bottom."

In BUA (Bottom-Up Approach), we test the integration starting with the Core Services layer and add one more layer on top of it until we fully cover the system.

Let's try to build a test suite for our calendar feature (Figure 5-6).

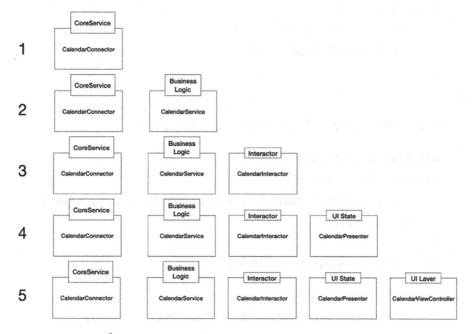

Figure 5-6. *BUA test suite for the calendar feature*

The preceding diagram describes the list of tests we write to come up with incremental testing to our feature. As you can see, we are adding one test in each step. Just like standard unit tests, it is recommended that you test each step in a test method of its own to separate your tests from each other.

Let's take a look at how it's done in code:

```
class CalendarConnectorSpy : CalendarConnectorProtocol {

    var fetchEventsFromDate : Date?
    var fetchEventsToDate : Date?

    func fetchEvents(fromDate startDate: Date, toDate endDate:
    Date, visibleCalendars: [String]) -> [EventItem] {
        return []
    }

    func clean() {
        fetchEventsFromDate = nil
        fetchEventsToDate = nil
    }
}

class CalendarScreenIntegrationTests: XCTestCase {

    var startDate : Date = Date()
    var endDate : Date = {
        return Calendar.current.date(byAdding: .hour, value: 1,
        to: Date())!
    }()
    let spy = CalendarConnectorSpy()

    override func setUp() {
        CalendarService.shared.calendarConnector = spy
    }

    override func tearDown() {
        CalendarService.shared.calendarConnector =
        CalendarConnector()
        spy.clean()
    }
```

```swift
    func validateDates(file : StaticString = #file, line : UInt
    = #line) {
        XCTAssertEqual(spy.fetchEventsFromDate!, startDate)
        XCTAssertEqual(spy.fetchEventsToDate!, endDate)
    }

// ------ testing the bottom layers ---------
    func testBusinessLogicLayer() {
        // arrange and act
        _ = CalendarService.shared.fetchEvents(fromDate:
        startDate, toDate: endDate)

        // assert
        validateDates()
    }

// ----   adding the interactor -------
    func testInteractorLayer() {
        // arrange
        let interactor = CalendarScreenInteractor()

        // act
        _ = interactor.fetchEvents(fromDate: startDate, toDate:
        endDate)

        // assert
        validateDates()
    }

// ------ reaching to the UI Login layer
    func testPresenterLayer() {
        // arrange
        let presenter = CalendarScreenPresenter()
```

```
        // act
        presenter.onDateChange(toDate: startDate)

        // assert
        validateDates()
    }

// ---------- this is the top layer ---------
    func testVCLayer() {
        // arrange
        let vc = CalendarScreenViewController(nibName:
        "CalendarScreenViewController", bundle: nil)
        vc.loadViewIfNeeded()

        // act
        vc.tappedDate(date: startDate)

        // assert
        validateDates()()
    }
}
```

Let's start with the **setUp()** and **tearDown()** methods:

```
override func setUp() {
        CalendarService.shared.calendarConnector = spy
    }

    override func tearDown() {
        CalendarService.shared.gConnector = CalendarConnector()
        spy.clean()
    }
```

In calendar features, it's hard to run a broad integration test, mainly because it requires user permissions to the calendar itself.

So, in this case, we create a **spy**. If you recall, a spy is an object that doesn't return anything, but instead, it records calls and information.

We connect our spy to our CalendarService singleton, and on the teardown() method, we clean it up.

Our first test is related to the next layer after the connector layer – the CalendarService layer:

```
func validateDates(file : StaticString = #file, line : UInt
= #line) {
    XCTAssertEqual(spy.fetchEventsFromDate!, startDate)
    XCTAssertEqual(spy.fetchEventsToDate!, endDate)
}

func testBusinessLogicLayer() {
    // arrange and act
    _ = CalendarService.shared.fetchEvents(fromDate:
    startDate, toDate: endDate)

    // assert
    validateDates()
}
```

In our test method, we run the CalendarService method (fetchEvents()), and hopefully, it will fill our spy with useful information.

In order not to repeat ourselves in each test, we create a custom assertion method to validate the dates the spy receives, just like we've learned in previous chapters.

After our business logic test passed, we can continue to the next layer – the screen interactor:

```
func testInteractorLayer() {
    // arrange
    let interactor = CalendarScreenInteractor()
```

```
// act
_ = interactor.fetchEvents(fromDate: startDate, toDate:
endDate)

// assert
validateDates()
}
```

Same goes in here – we call the fetchEvents() method in the interactor and check the spy at the end.

We continue with the test until we reach the last layer – the UIViewController.

In this layer, we simulate the user action:

```
vc.tappedDate(date: startDate)
```

The Bottom-Up approach is easy to implement and reduces the use of test doubles. However, using the Bottom-Up approach is not possible, and you have to go with **Top-Down** Incremental testing.

Top-Down

There are cases when the bottom layers are not ready yet. In fact, this is the usual situation when starting with the development of a new feature. We start by defining the interfaces between all layers and then continue to develop it top to bottom.

As we make progress in our development, we want to make sure our components are integrated correctly. Since our bottom layers are not ready yet, we can create a **stub** to replace them and, by that, create incremental tests on the go. This approach is called "Top-Down," and it is usually the approach we take during development when there are components that are not ready yet.

Dealing with the Edges

The most complicated steps in Integration Tests are the first and last –
simulating the UI behavior on one side and checking the results on the
other side, which may involve dealing with system frameworks, network,
and maybe a persistent store.

There are some solutions to those parts.

On the UI side, it is a best practice to **avoid calling directly to UI-**
related methods such as UIScrollView delegate methods or UITableView
dataSource. One solution is to take out the logic from those methods and
put it in pure functions.

In more complex UI screens, you might **consider eliminating the UI
layer** and only test the presenter/ViewModel classes. It is better to have
a narrower test than striving with a hard-to-maintain test that has more
chances to break in future changes.

On the core services side, avoid including layers that require user
permissions such as Calendar, Contacts, and Assets Library. Invest time in
fake and record data instead of finding hacks to bypass access permissions
(and there are some techniques for that).

Remember, although it is better to use the actual objects and simulate
a real-life flow, it is not worth spending a tremendous amount of time
bypassing and hacking the system for that.

Client-Server Tests

One fact is well known – most mobile apps today work with some kind
of a back end. In fact, some of them are deeply dependent on a server to
perform their first day-to-day tasks.

If we said that integration between internal layers could break easily,
it's especially true when talking about integration between our client and a
server.

But testing integrations with the server might be complicated and can have several challenges and issues:

- **Hard to Set Up** – Yes, sending requests to the server may be easy, but writing the assertion part when you need to compare the response to the expected one might be cumbersome. There are long and complicated JSON responses that are just too difficult to write, not to mention maintaining them over time with all future changes.

- **Slow** – Unlike unit tests or even narrow integration tests, Client-Server testing involves working with a server, and as a result, it depends on a network connection and back-end resources. When running tens of client-server requests, this may be an issue.

- **It Can Be Fragile** – In continuation of the previous section, the dependency on a server can cause those tests to break easily. Also, the assertion part is not simple – sometimes, a simple change in the response, such as an extra field or a different timestamp, can fail our test without any justice.

- **Dependencies Between Tests** – We always say that tests shouldn't be dependent on each other. But how can we test a data sync method if we didn't test the login method first? Most likely, we have some order we need to run those tests, and this is contrary to what we do in almost any other test.

Before we move on with Client-Server testing, we need to understand what exactly is the scope of our tests.

For instance, do we care about the structure of the response, or do we just need to make sure our client processes it correctly?

If we get an HTTP 200 status code, is it enough for our test to pass?

As you can tell, it is vital to narrow down what exactly we are going to test and what's important to us.

In general, it is accepted that client-server tests are divided into two main approaches – Black Box and White Box Testing (Figure 5-7).

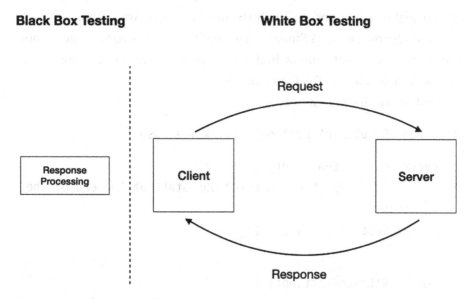

Figure 5-7. *Black Box vs. White Box Testing*

Black Box testing ignores structures and protocol and focuses on behavior only. White Box testing validates the protocols, structure, requests, and responses. These are entirely two approaches, and the decision on what to choose is crucial.

Note   Black Box and White Box are being used in many test areas and not just in Client-Server. You can meet these terms especially when talking about UI Testing.

Black Box Client-Server Testing

In Black Box testing, we don't care about the actual request and response. We don't deal with JSON's or any other data structure. What we do care is the **functionality**.

When talking about Client-Server Testing, the Black Box approach is more straightforward and probably the most common way to go.

So, where do we start? Since we are dealing with network requests, our tests have to be asynchronous. In this case, we're going to use a tool we previously learned – XCTestExpectation.

Look at our first Client-Server test:

```
class LoginServiceIntegrationTests: XCTestCase {

    override func tearDown() {
        // it's important to reset our state at the end of the
        test
        LoginService().logout()
    }

    func testLoginFunction() {
        // we define our expectation and a local variable to
        store the incoming result
        let expectation = self.expectation(description: "Check
        Login Flow Message")
        var receivedResult : LoginOperationResult = .success

        LoginService().doLogin(email: "avi@myemail.com",
        password: "123") { (result) in
            receivedResult = result
            expectation.fulfill()
        }
```

```
    // since it's a network request, we wait 10 seconds to make
    sure we are getting an answer even in slow connection
    self.waitForExpectations(timeout: 10.0, handler: nil)

    // assert
    XCTAssertEqual(receivedResult, LoginOperationResult.
    success)

    }
}
```

In the preceding example, we test our login mechanism. As you can see, we need to use a constant user name and password.

As alternative, we can chain two requests – Registration and Login:

```
func testRegistrationService() {
    // we define our expectation and a local variable to
    store the incoming result
    let expectation = self.expectation(description: "Check
    Register and Login Flow")
    var receivedResult : LoginOperationResult = .failure

    let email = generateEmail()
    let password = generatePassword()

    RegisterService().register(email: email
    , password: password) { (result) in

        if result == .success {
            LoginService().doLogin(email: email, password:
            password) { (loginResult) in
                receivedResult = loginResult
                expectation.fulfill()

            }
        }
    }
```

```
    // since it's a network request, we wait 10 seconds
    to make sure we are getting an answer even in slow
    connection
    self.waitForExpectations(timeout: 15.0, handler: nil)

    // assert
    XCTAssertEqual(receivedResult, LoginOperationResult.
    success)
}
```

We generate an email and password, create a new user, and then try to log in with the same credentials. As mentioned before, unlike other test categories, client-server testing sometimes requires chaining requests together. In many situations, Integration tests simulate real user flow scenarios, so planning your tests is a little different than standard unit tests.

Also, remember that Client-Server tests not only influence the state of your app but also on the data in your server. So, cleaning after your tests is a crucial step.

White Box Client-Server Testing

Black Box testing is excellent.

It's easier to write because you don't have to deal with test doubles. You are not "dirtying" your hands with parsing server response and comparing values. Also, usually, black box tests cover the essential things and basic functionality.

But Black Box testing has its drawbacks. There are cases when checking only your functionality is not enough, cases where you need a more profound validation and test the structure of your request and response.

Data sync is a good example – we send a sync request and receive a success response. But is it enough to determine that our integration works well? What if we didn't send all the expected data? What if we needed to send a critical flag or essential piece of data, but our request was missing this piece of data?

White Box Integration aims to fill that gap. In white box integration, we go deeper into our testing and check the protocols between our client and the server.

The process of creating a white box testing is built upon three steps:

Bring your app to an ideal state, a state that defined the baseline. From now on, you're going to compare your tests to this state.

Snapshot that state – record your requests and responses and save them to a file. We can call the saved responses "Gold Responses" because those are the ideal responses we should get when we run our tests.

In your tests, **execute your logic functions**, but this time, record (again) your requests and responses and, in the end, compare them to the gold responses you saved in the early step.

While these steps might sound scary, building an excellent infrastructure and helpers can help you achieve them.

Bring Your App to an Ideal State

Sure, we can implement TDD with this process. But TDD is great when defining behaviors in advance. When checking data structures, it is simpler and easier to do it while "snapshotting" an ideal state that we reached. By the way, in my opinion, it's not a wrong approach when writing tests other than unit tests.

Record the Current State

To record our requests and responses, we need to create some network recorder. The network recorder receives the request and the response, bundles them together, and saves them to a file (Figure 5-8).

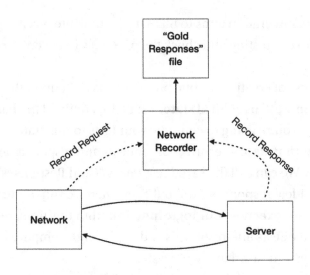

Figure 5-8. *Implementing a network recorder*

The interface of such a recorder is simple:

```
typealias RequestData = [AnyHashable : Any]
typealias ResponseDate = [AnyHashable : Any]

struct RequestBundle {
    var request : RequestData
    var response : ResponseDate
}

enum RequestBundleType {
    case login
    case register
    case sync
    case setup
}
```

```
class NetworkRecorder {

    var data = [RequestBundleType : RequestBundle]()

    func recordRequest(bundle : RequestBundle, type :
    RequestBundleType) {
        // save the bundle to data
    }

    private func saveDataToFile(data : [RequestBundleType :
    RequestBundle]) {
        // save the data into a file.
    }
}
```

To activate recording, we can use the launch arguments that we've already learned in previous chapters (Figure 5-9).

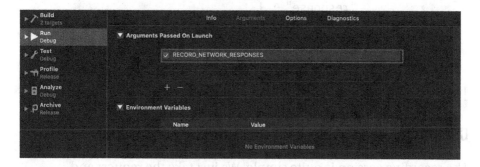

***Figure 5-9.** Launch Arguments to activate recording*

All we need to do after the snapshotting session is to take the "Gold Responses" file and add it to our test bundle so we can validate our requests and responses in the future.

The gold responses file can look something like this:

```
[
    {
            "request" : "login_request",
            "response" : {
                    "id" : "f3e0b3a7-6db7-408e-bd26-
                    a91bf31c03d2",
                    "name" : "Avi Tsadok",
                    "token" : "peoqFB8KcAjmVtQfe34TmWxgpum
                               IUEhs",
                    "updated_date" : "1589603996"
            }
    },
    {
            "request" :            "configuration",
            "response" : {
                    "push_notification_on" : 1
            }
    }
]
```

Comparing Responses with the Gold Responses File

The recording session is quite simple. We just take the request and response and put it in a file. But the real challenge is the comparison.

First, I must say these white box tests are very fragile. Every small, harmless change in the structure or values can make our tests to fail. Keep that in mind, and make sure you implement those tests on critical use cases such as sync and login.

Nevertheless, if we do decide to write white box testing, there are some issues we need to take into consideration:

- The data type that usually causes problems is **Date/ Time** or, in other words, **Timestamps**. These values are often driven from the computer time or server time. There are several ways to deal with it:

  - Sometimes it's important to fail the test **if the timestamp is incorrect**.

  - Sometimes, the timestamp is **relative**. In this case, we need to adapt our comparison also to be relative.

  - In most cases, it is better to **ignore** any comparison to the values, but just make sure it is present.

- We need to decide what to do if the response or the request contains additional values that are not present in the gold responses file. Usually, extra attributes are harmless to your code, and you can ignore them.

- If your response contains arrays, you need to decide if the order of the elements is crucial.

As you can see, the comparison method you need to write can be complicated. The cost of writing white box client-server integration tests is much higher than a black box and can break easily.

Summary

While Integration Tests are important, they are harder to write and maintain. It is better to write integration tests to the critical parts of your app, and this is especially true when talking about Client-Server tests. Those tests improve not only your confidence in your code but in your system.

In the next chapter, we'll do a step backward and learn how to prepare our code for testing – both integration and unit tests.

CHAPTER 6

Write Testable Code

Quality means doing it right even when no one is looking.

—Henry Ford

Introduction

We already know that testing your app is a crucial task to maintain high-quality code over time. But to do that, we need our tests to be simple and easy.

Testable code is a derivative of robust, modular architecture and clean, simple code. Although this chapter does not deal directly with testing, it's a prerequisite to learn how to test your code, and in general, it's a good chance to leverage your code quality.

In this chapter, you will learn

- What is **Clean Code**, including terms like KISS, DRY, and YAGNI

- What are **Pure Functions** and how it can help your code to be more testable

- The different ways to implement **Dependency Injection**

- What are **SOLID** principles

© Avi Tsadok 2020
A. Tsadok, *Pro iOS Testing*, https://doi.org/10.1007/978-1-4842-6382-2_6

- Design Patterns that you can use to organize your code, including **Singleton, Façade, Decorator, and Factory**

- What are **MVC, MVP, MVVM, and VIPER** and which one is better for your needs

What Is a Testable Code?

Testable code is a code you don't need to struggle with writing automated tests for. In most cases, it also means high-quality, simple, and readable code.

Look at the following code from the main screen of our great My Weather app:

```
override func  viewDidAppear(_ animated: Bool) {
super.viewDidAppear(animated)

    var request = URLRequest(url: URL(string: "http://www.
    myweatherapp.com/getCities.php")!)
    request.httpMethod = "GET"
    let task = networkSession.dataTask(with: request)
    {(data, response, error) in
        if let receivedData = data {
            try receivedData.write(to: self.localURL)
        }
    }
    task.resume()
}
```

Let's summarize what this code snippet does:

- Runs when the screen appeared

- Creates a GET request

- Creates a data task to send the request

- Writes the received data from the GET request to a local file

While it may seem like a simple code, it is unlikely to be testable from the following reasons:

- All the code **is inside the ViewDidAppear method**. This method is part of the UIViewController life cycle and potentially contains more code not related to downloading files. Also, we may want to move this code out in the future and put it in another method. This step can cause our tests to fail when doing that.

- The code sends an HTTP request to our server. While in some integration tests this is acceptable, we don't want to rely on an Internet connection or server state in our unit and BDD tests (not even in some UI Tests). We can't let **server or network issues** affect the result of our tests, and in this example, it is difficult to mock our requests.

- In case of success, the code writes data to a file. Checking if the file is written is excellent for integration tests, less for unit tests. Having a function with **a side effect** is less convenient to test, especially if it involves I/O operations.

But don't worry! There are a couple of things we can do to improve our code.

First, we can remove the code from the viewDidAppear method and put it in its own function. Second, we can create two service layers, **NetworkClient** to handle network requests and **DataLayer** to handle I/O operations.

143

Look at the following fixed code:

```
override func  viewDidAppear(_ animated: Bool) {
    super.viewDidAppear(animated)
    loadCities()
}

func loadCities() {
    NetworkClient.shared.fetchCities {(data) in
        if let receivedData = data {
            DataLayer().saveCitiesData(data: receivedData)
        }
    }
}
```

Now our code is much cleaner, easy to read, and, yes, more testable. You can test loadCities() function; without worry, it might contain unrelated logic, and it's straightforward to mock all the other dependencies.

We can say that writing clean and modular code is not only a higher-quality code, but it's also a more testable one. Testable code and high-quality code naturally go hand in hand, and this is what this chapter is all about.

Clean Code

There are plenty of great books discussing clean Code. The primary excuse for not writing a clean and structured Code is "not enough time." Well, writing a clean Code doesn't mean "more time." Not only that, but cleaner code can also actually save you time in the future while being easier to maintain and test. Clean Code is a matter of mindset.

There are several principles and guidelines for writing a clean Code, and I will go over some of them.

KISS (Keep It Simple, Stupid)

KISS states for "Keep It Simple, Stupid". KISS is not just the "One Rule to Rule Them All," but it's also the hardest rule to follow.

The root of the problem is human nature. When we write code, we understand it. We understand it the same day later and maybe even the day after.

But a few months later or even a few weeks later, when we look at our code, we find ourselves struggling to understand what we wrote.

Ironically, it's more common to see a dirty, complex code in a beginner's code. The reason is that writing a simple code is complicated. It takes a lot of experience and knowledge to write a simple, structural code, with clear function names, layers, and good, understandable API.

It also requires abstract thinking, technology understating, and mostly much maturity not to chase every new framework or language feature the minute they pop up.

But there are some rule thumbs for keeping your code simple.

> *Measuring programming progress by lines of code is like measuring aircraft building progress by weight.*
>
> —Bill Gates

Less is more: shorter functions, shorter classes, and shorter files. If your function takes more than 50 or 60 lines of code, it's a good sign for you to reconsider rewriting or splitting it.

The same goes for classes – they need to be short with no more than 20 methods. Imagine someone trying to read a class interface with 40–50 methods. Just like long methods, consider splitting it.

Less code is less code to read and, more importantly, less code to debug and test.

After 30 statements you have in your function, chances to have a bug increase. It becomes harder to cover all the states and output the function can produce.

The nature of big functions is to get bigger and bigger until they become code monsters that no one knows how they work, and everybody prays they won't break in the future.

Handle variables with care. If your code is like a "country," the variables are its "citizens." Don't give them meaningless names like "i" or "qty"; try names like "city" or "firstPersonInTheList". Think of your code as a story written in English, not Swift.

Keep your **variables' scope as small as possible**. Don't declare variables outside of a for loop when you only use them inside the loop. Try to avoid instance variables to float around your class if you can pass them as an argument to functions.

Don't reuse variables – if you have a string variable that was used to store a person's first name, don't reuse it to store last name or an email. This can cause you headaches, trying to understand what that variable represents at a specific statement.

Use **Typealias** when you can. Typealias is a great way to explain your code without the need for comments.

DRY

DRY stands for **Don't Repeat Yourself**, and it means that every piece of knowledge or logic you have in your app should be in one single place and not duplicated across your project. This can be either business logic code, network access, UI Component, or anything you think of that should be in one place and copied around your project. Code duplication is a common source for bugs or inconsistent behavior, and every developer knows that it is considered being bad practice.

YAGNI (You Aren't Gonna Need It)

YAGNI is another simplicity principle saying that you shouldn't develop a feature or be prepared for it unless you are going to use or need it.

There is an assumption that when a developer works on a feature, he should take into account potential future extensions to the feature and, as a result, to build a flexible architecture in the cost of simplicity and readability.

This assumption is based on the idea that building a system at the thought of future changes is more cost-effective than doing those changes later.

The problem is that the cost estimation doesn't include maintenance over time, more complicated tests to support it, and a much more complex system to work with. It's much more comfortable and cost-effective to write simple code that works and refactor when the time comes.

I'm not saying **don't** write flexible architectures – but in most cases, future features that we don't know what they are and if they will come are not developed at all. In the meantime, this complex system that we built has cost us with extra maintenance we don't need.

Code That Is Pleasant to Read Is Also Pleasant to Test

I mentioned before that quality and testability go hand in hand. Pleasant to read code is also easier to test. The primary thumb rule for knowing if your code is readable is comments. If you overuse comments, this can be a good sign, something is wrong with your code, and it may be too complicated to understand.

Swift has some great tools to help you make your code more delightful.

I mentioned **Typealias** before as a way to write the names of a descriptive and meaningful variable, but there are more ways to make your code look more delicate.

147

For example, instead of writing a function with lots of arguments, it is better to **pass a struct bundling** them together.

Take a look at the following code:

```
func runRegistrationProcess(email : String, name : String,
password : String, receivingEmailApproval : Bool) {

}
```

Now it can look like this:

```
struct RegistrationData {
    var email                  :    String
    var name                   :    String
    var password               :    String
    var receivingEmailApproval :    Bool
}

func runRegistrationProcess(registrationData :
RegistrationData) {

}
```

Nice, isn't it? Also, it's better for testing, because it makes the API much more clear and predefined, and those arguments can be quickly passed forward to more functions and objects.

Another way to make your code more beautiful is to define your **code style and naming conventions**. Code Style (indentations, empty lines between methods, variables order, and more) is not only for the look. When you keep your code's structure constant, it makes your code scanning much more comfortable and makes use of the short-term memory better. It can help you read old code better and make your debug session much easier. It doesn't matter what code style you choose as long as you keep it constant throughout your project.

Of course, all the principles given also refer to the testing code. You should treat your tests as a "Real" code and not just a playground for your app. Testing code is also a code you need to maintain and debug overtime.

Pure Functions

This is another way to make our code more testable and clean.

One of the key factors for testing is the ability to run your tests over and over again with the same arguments and expect the same behavior at each run.

To reach a very stable testing bundle, we need our tests to be **isolated** from any external state, both for input and for output. One of the problems we have in object-oriented programming is that its encapsulation nature encourages us to use instance variables inside our functions, which kind of is missing the point of isolation.

Pure Functions are functions that don't generate any side effects or do not depend on the external state like global or instance variables in a way that you always get the same output for the same input.

To achieve that, we want to pass all the required data using the function's arguments, including the instance variables. Take a look at Figure 6-1.

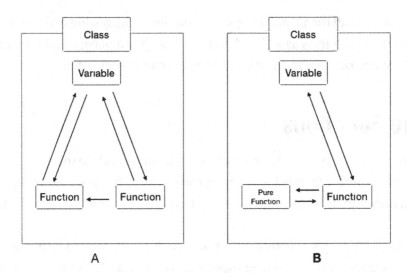

Figure 6-1. *Pure Function vs. Standard function*

The class displayed in diagram A doesn't have any pure functions. It has one function that makes use of other functions, and they both work with instance variables. By looking at Figure 6-1, you can understand that those functions are not "pure". This means those functions have side effects, and they are based on an instance variable.

To test those functions, you need to make sure this instance variable is set to a specific value before you start the test itself.

Setting up the initial state before each test run can lead to complicated test functions, with a high chance of breaking them in the future.

Now let's take a look at the diagram B (still, Figure 6-1). You can see that the described pure function is not working with any instance or global variable and therefore always produces the same results for the same arguments.

This is also true for calling system and SDK framework since they also potentially hold their own state.

Refactor Our Functions to Be Pure

One thumb rule you can use to check if your function is pure is to move it to another class. If you have to modify the function implementation to use it, good chances are it's not pure. Pure functions need to be not only class agnostic but also SDK agnostic.

Take a look at the method updateTitle(:) in CitiesViewController:

```
class CitiesViewController: UIViewController {

    var topTitle : String?
    var placeType: String = "City"

    override func viewDidLoad() {
        super.viewDidLoad()
        updateTitle(newTitle: "New York")
    }

    func updateTitle(newTitle : String) {
        self.topTitle = String(format: "%@ - %@", placeType,
        newTitle.uppercased())
    }
}
```

It seems like a straightforward code – updateTitle(:) is getting one argument and sets the top title according to the new title and placeType instance variable. You can already understand that this method is not pure. The method is based on an instance variable in the input side and updates another instance variable on the output side.

The good news is that it's really easy to refactor the code and change this function to be pure:

```
class CitiesViewController: UIViewController {

    var topTitle : String?
    var placeType : String = "City"
```

```
override func viewDidLoad() {
    super.viewDidLoad()
    topTitle = updateTitle(newTitle: "New York", placeType:
    placeType)
}

func updateTitle(newTitle : String, placeType : String)
->String {
    return String(format: "%@ - %@", placeType, newTitle.
    uppercased())
}
}
```

In the refactored code, you can see I added another argument to the function called "placeType" and that the method no longer changes the instance variable; instead, it returns the new value.

While this may look like a small change, it makes the function totally pure. This isolation means that tests for this function are very easy to set up.

To summarize pure function:

- It is better to try and make your functions return a value instead of updating an instance or a global variable.

- Try to pass arguments to the function instead of preventing it from accessing your instance variables, other frameworks, or singletons.

- The best way to check if your function is pure is to try and move it to another place in your code. If you can still use it, it's probably pure.

Protocol-Oriented Programming

The main advantage of using Protocols instead of basic OOP (object-oriented programming) is that a class can conform to multiple protocols. This ability allows us to design a very flexible and modular architecture. This ensures transparent and predictable behavior, which is very important for building tests.

When you design your architecture, try to make your layers connect with each other only through protocols. Take a look at Figure 6-2.

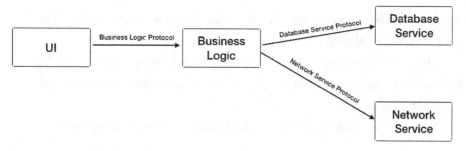

Figure 6-2. Protocol-oriented programming

Protocols are the "glue" that connects the objects in your architecture. This flexibility is reflected by the fact that you can replace each object in your system with a new one as long as it conforms to the required protocol. Replacing objects easily is really handy when we talk about mocking layers and behaviors.

Dependency Injection

One of the problems when talking about isolation is the dependencies between layers and objects in your code. We know, for example, that UI components are based on some business logic components. The business logic components are also dependent on some core services such as network and database layers.

153

When we want to test a method in one of those layers, we sometimes find ourselves struggling to adjust those methods' behavior to the one that can help us achieve the task efficiently. Remember, again, if it's too hard to test it, it might be a good sign that your code isn't easy enough to maintain over time.

But there is a way to control the behavior of an object by **injecting** its instance variables – it's called **Dependency Injection**.

Ways to Implement Dependency Injection

Now, let's go back to Dependency Injection and see how it is related to protocol-oriented programming.

There are several patterns to implement Dependency Injection. There isn't a "best way" or "correct way"; it all depends on your situation and your personal flavor.

Take a look at the following "CitiesManager" business logic unit:

```
class CitiesManager {

    func refreshCitiesFromServer() {
        NetworkClient.shared.fetchCities {[weak self] (data) in
            if data != nil {
                self?.saveCitiesDataToDisk(data: data!)
            }
        }
    }

    private func saveCitiesDataToDisk(data : Data) {
        DatabaseClient.shared.saveCitiesDataToDB(data: data)
    }
}
```

In refreshCitiesFromServer, the code calls the network client, received its data, and then saves it to disk. Although this function is minimal, it's still hard to test. "NetworkClient" opens HTTP requests, and "DatabaseClient" is doing I/O operations. We can safely say this class is dependent on these two objects.

The first way of injecting other dependencies is using its constructor.

The Classic One – Initializer-Based DI

The Initializer-based Dependency Injection is a way to give the object its dependencies when it's being initialized (I guess you knew that from its name). This is done by writing a constructor that receives the required dependencies in its arguments.

Let's take the CitiesManager class from the last example and try to refactor it:

```
class CitiesManager {

    var dataBaseClient : DatabaseClientProtocol
    var networkClient : NetworkClientProtocol

    init(databaseClient : DatabaseClientProtocol =
    DatabaseClient.shared, networkClient :
    NetworkClientProtocol = NetworkClient.shared) {
        self.dataBaseClient = databaseClient
        self.networkClient = networkClient
    }

    func refreshCitiesFromServer() {
        networkClient.fetchCities {[weak self] (data) in
            if data != nil {
                self?.saveCitiesDataToDisk(data: data!)
            }
        }
    }
}
```

```
    private func saveCitiesDataToDisk(data : Data) {
        dataBaseClient.saveCitiesDataToDB(data: data)
    }
}
```

There are two important things we did here:

- We **created a new constructor**, which expects to receive two dependencies – the database client and the network client.

- Those dependencies are **protocol based**, meaning we can inject any objects that we want as long as it conforms to the required protocol.

The big advantage of this approach is that it requires us to inject external dependencies, and that ensures that the class behaves the way we want.

The Simple Way – Property-Based DI

Another way to inject dependencies is Property-Based injection, which is also the simplest way.

In Property-Based injection, we assigned the dependencies after the object has been initialized:

```
class CitiesManager {

    var dataBaseClient : DatabaseClientProtocol = DatabaseClient.
    shared
    var networkClient : NetworkClientProtocol = NetworkClient.
    shared

    func refreshCitiesFromServer() {
        networkClient.fetchCities {[weak self] (data) in
            if data != nil {
```

```
                self?.saveCitiesDataToDisk(data: data!)
            }
        }
    }

    private func saveCitiesDataToDisk(data : Data) {
        dataBaseClient.saveCitiesDataToDB(data: data)
    }
}

let citiesManager = CitiesManager()
// Setting the dependencies
citiesManager.dataBaseClient = myCustomDatabaseClient
citiesManager.networkClient = myCustomNetworkClient
```

You need to be aware that property-based injection has upsides and downsides. For example, it is much simpler to implement than the initializer way, and it can be convenient when **subclassing or doing that on a XIB-based view**.

It also **doesn't require you to refactor existing constructors**, which can be quite a headache in many projects and let you easily add new dependencies to an existing class.

But Property-Based injection also has some downsides. It requires you to **expose instant variables** when all you want is to assign them. Another consideration is that the injection **is not part of any interface** the compiler can assure or notifies us, so you may not know what the dependencies are or how to inject them.

The Compromised Way – Parameter-Based DI

The Parameter-Based way doesn't require you to change your constructor signature or expose your instance variables. The idea behind Parameter-Based DI is to inject the dependencies only to the method you call using its arguments:

```
class CitiesManager {

    func refreshCitiesFromServer(networkClient :
    NetworkClientProtocol = NetworkClient.shared,
    dataBaseClient : DatabaseClientProtocol = DatabaseClient.
    shared) {
        networkClient.fetchCities {[weak self] (data) in
            if data != nil {
                self?.saveCitiesDataToDisk(data: data!)
            }
        }
    }

    private func saveCitiesDataToDisk(data : Data,
    dataBaseClient : DatabaseClientProtocol = DatabaseClient.
    shared) {
        dataBaseClient.saveCitiesDataToDB(data: data)
    }
}

let citiesManager = CitiesManager()
citiesManager.refreshCitiesFromServer(networkClient:
myCustomNetworkClient, dataBaseClient: myCustomDatabaseClient)
```

Not only you don't expose your instance variables; in many cases, you do **not even have dependencies as instance variables**. The Parameter-Based injection can help you make your functions pure, which can make your testing much easier.

SOLID Principles

SOLID is an acronym that represents five important design principles that can help you write understandable and easier to maintain code and, as a result, a more testable one.

Following these principles is not hard, but it requires you to pay attention whenever you decide to create a new method.

Let's go over them.

S – Single-Responsibility Principle

This means an object should do one thing and should be the only object in your project that does this thing. It's harder to maintain methods and classes that are responsible for several things, and breaking them is just a matter of time. For example, if your method parses a network response and writes to the disk, split it into two methods and test them separately.

O – Open/Closed Principle

A class should be open to extension but closed to change. Whenever you're done writing a method/class and testing it, consider it closed. If you need to add its behavior, do it by subclassing, dependency injection, or using Swift extensions (or Objective-C Categories). This will help you decrease the number of test's rewrites every time you need to change something and also help you avoid regressions.

L – Liskov Substitution Principle

LSP (Liskov Substitution Principle) may be hard to understand at first, but it's very simple to implement, so try to concentrate here ☺. What LSP means is that if type A is dependent upon type B, then objects of type B may be replaced with objects of type A. In other words, subclass objects should keep the behavior of the superclasses in any matter.

Let's try to understand it using the next example:

```
protocol ChatMessage {

    var sender : String { get set }
    var content : String { get set }
    var time : Date { get set }
    var fileURL : URL { get set }
}

struct TextMessage : ChatMessage {

}

struct AudioMessage : ChatMessage {

}

struct ImageMessage : ChatMessage
{

}

struct FileMessage : ChatMessage {

}
```

In the preceding example, we tried to design a basic structure for a chat system. We created a protocol named ChatMessage and four different struct types that conform to this protocol.

The protocol assumes that all structs have some fileURL data, but this is not true – the fileURL is not relevant for TextMessage struct. The same goes for the content variable – it's only relevant for TextMessage but not for the others. Some may say "So what? I can just ignore and return an empty string or empty URL." Of course, it can be done, but remember the code that is going to use TextMessage **expects the fileURL to contain a real value**; otherwise, it wouldn't be there. The solution, in this case, is to split the protocols:

```
protocol ChatMessage {

    var sender : String { get set }
    var time : Date { get set }
}

protocol ChatMessageFile {
    var fileURL : URL { get set }
}

protocol ChatMessageTextual {
        var content : String { get set }
}

struct TextMessage : ChatMessage, ChatMessageTextual {

}

struct AudioMessage : ChatMessage, ChatMessageFile {

}

struct ImageMessage : ChatMessage, ChatMessageFile
{

}

struct FileMessage : ChatMessage, ChatMessageFile {

}
```

You follow this principle also for subclassing. When overriding method from the superclass, if you don't call the superclass method, you are actually violating the LSP and may remove a critical behavior.

To summarize it, always call the superclass method and always implement the required protocol methods. If they are not relevant, you are probably doing something wrong; consider splitting or changing architecture.

I – Interface-Segregation Principle

The previous principle is built upon the Interface-Segregation Principle. The basic rule here is creating the minimal interface you need for objects and structs. This is also true also for class public methods and also for protocols. When a class needs to implement methods it uses, it requires your mock objects to implement those methods as well. This adds levels of complexity to your project and your tests. Create small protocols – it will pay off for you in the future.

D – Dependency Inversion Principle

The Dependency Inversion Principle is a form of decoupling software modules. The principle states

1. High-level modules should not depend on low-level modules. Both should depend on abstractions.

2. Abstractions should not depend on details. Details should depend on abstractions.

In other words, when high-level objects interact with lower-level objects, they do not need to know their implementation or even their class, but only their interface. This can be done using abstraction (Protocol or Base class) and reducing coupling.

Also, when designing an abstraction, it needs to be done from the point of **what are the goals** of this abstraction and not **how** it is going to implement them. The best technique to do that is to design first your architecture UML (Unified Modeling Language) and then write it as a protocol in your code. Only then you build your classes and start coding.

Decoupling your architecture is actually what testing is based on. The ability to exchange each part in your system with another object **as long as it conforms** to the defined abstraction is important for mocking and molding your initial testing state.

Design Patterns and Architectures

Design Pattern is a reusable solution you can apply to a common problem you have in your project. The problem can be network requests, a screen, communication between objects, and more. An example of such a design pattern can be a **delegate**.

Some design patterns solve UI problems or some database access problems; there isn't a "right" design pattern but rather a design pattern that fits your need.

All design patterns have cons and pros, and they have a deep influence on your ability to cover your app with tests.

Singleton

A Singleton is a case when you have only one copy of a class. The reference to the one instance of the class is done using a static variable that points to this instance.

While it is very convenient to create and use a singleton, they are overused in many projects. Overuse of a singleton is not a best practice, not only in terms of memory but mostly in control.

Use the Singleton pattern only if you need **one and only one** instance of your class. One good example is a network handler or a database connector, because in both cases, it's inefficient to hold multiple connections or requests.

Also, a class that contains a state of something should have one and only one instance to avoid data conflicts.

Creating a singleton is very easy, and you can do that with one line only:

```
class NetworkClient {

    static let shared = NetworkClient()
```

```
    private init() {

    }

}

let networkClient = NetworkClient.shared
```

Writing tests that involve singletons should not be a major problem. You should be able to mock singletons easily and make use of them using dependency injection covered earlier.

Note   It's important to note at this point that most of the described design patterns here are based on principles you learned in this chapter. As long as you are following those principles, choosing the right design pattern should be easy and intuitive.

Facade

Facade is a simple interface that hides a complex system of classes. The Facade is used when you have a set of classes, and you want to put them under the same "umbrella" since they are all related to each other in some way.

For example, let's go back to our Weather app. We have a class that handles login, a class that handles registration, and a class that handles the mechanism of "forget password."

On the one hand, it seems good we separated this logic to multiple classes, but on the other hand, it's getting much more complicated now, since our authentication logic is spread across three different classes.

So, we can create a Facade – one unified interface that can help you access your public methods from one place.

Let's take a look of such Facade:

```
class UserAccessFacade {

    lazy private var loginService = LoginService()
    lazy private var registerService = RegisterService()
    lazy private var forgetPasswordService =
    ForgetPasswordService()

    func doLogin(email : String, password : String) {
        loginService.doLogin(email: email, password: password)
    }

    func doRegister(email : String, password: String, name :
    String) {
        registerService.doRegister(email: email, password:
        password, name: name)
    }

    func doForgetPassword(email : String) {
        forgetPasswordService.doForgetPassword(email: email)
    }

}
```

The Facade holds the relevant objects as private and has a simple interface to the relevant methods. The developer that uses the Facade is not aware of the complexity underneath.

In terms of testing, Facade is very testable as it lets you replace the whole object inside it and still maintains its behavior while keeping its interface constant.

Decorator

Decorator is a popular design pattern that modifies the behavior of an object without changing its interface or its code.

The Decorator is an object that wraps the core object and has the same interface. The Decorator acts as a "middleman" and by that can "decorate" the behavior of the original object.

The Decorator is useful in situations when you cannot or don't want to change the code of an existing class. Frameworks and legacy code are good examples of a situation like that.

For the "client" that uses a Decorator, it doesn't matter if it works with the original class or a decorator since they both use the same interface.

Another way to decorate an object other than wrapping it is to use Swift extensions or Objective-C Categories. Both are good examples for not modifying an existing code but expanding it.

Factory

Factory is a design pattern that encapsulates the object creation process. It implements several principles, like single responsibility and isolation.

The basic form of a Factory is an object that creates other objects – for example, if you have a table view with different kinds of cells, you can create a cell factory to create those cells according to their corresponding object models.

But Factory can do more than that – it can decide **what type** of object to return based on the arguments it gets. Let's say we want to create a car factory that produces a car according to a customer needs:

```
struct Mazda : Car {

}

struct Toyota : Car {

}

struct BMW : Car {

}
```

```
class CarsFactory {

    func getCar(accordingTo customerNeeds : CustomerNeeds)->Car
{
        switch customerNeeds.typeRequested {
        case .mazda:
            return Mazda()
        case .toyota:
            return Toyota()
        case .bmw:
            return BMW()
        }
    }
}
```

As you can see from the preceding code, the CarsFactory encapsulates the logic of the decision what type of struct to return by examining the received customer needs. The caller for the getCar method doesn't care about the implementation as long as it gets a "Car" back. This way, we can write the logic in one place only and test it easily while it's isolated nicely from the rest of the codebase.

MVC

Important   Since this book is about testing and not architectures, I only want to go over the next parts in general to make you move to more testable design patterns. Many books are discussing these topics, and I recommend you invest some time studying it in case MVC, MVVM, MVP, and VIPER are strange words for you.

One of the first things junior developers struggle with is responsibilities' distribution or, in simple words, "Where do I put this code snippet?" question.

The MVC pattern is considered to be the simplest pattern to follow, and Apple itself recommends it.

MVC stands for Model-View-Controller, and it is common not only in Apple development environments but in other platforms as well.

Although MVC is not the best pattern for tests to be based on, it's still quite popular, and you should know how to make it testable as much as you can. Also, MVC is what the other patterns are based on, so knowing it better can help you work with more sophisticated design patterns in the future.

So, what is MVC (Model-View-Controller)? It's a design pattern that separates the business logic and data ("Model") from the UI ("View"), while the Controller is the "glue" between them.

To understand how the interaction between the components works, take a look at Figure 6-3.

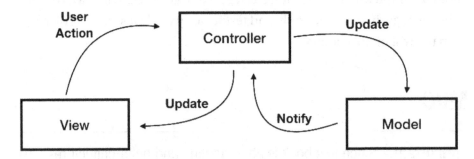

Figure 6-3. *MVC pattern*

If you notice, the Model and the View don't interact with each other. In real MVC pattern, the Model and the View don't even have a reference to each other, and all the interaction happens with the controller.

Here are examples of a flow to demonstrate it:

- The user taps a button (the View is sending the action to the controller).

- The app makes a network request. The controller decides to get the information and asks for the network layer (which represents the Model in this case) to make a request.

- The network layer (again, the Model in this case) makes the request and returns the results to the controller.

- The controller updates the TableView (which is also a part of the View) with new data.

From the flow described earlier, it's clear that the View layer (Button and TableView) doesn't become aware of the Model (Network Layer), and the controller acts as the middleman here.

But when we develop an app, what exactly are Model, View, and Controller?

The Model – M

The Model layers hold the app's data, but not only that. There are many examples of the Model layer:

- **Network Layer** - Usually a singleton, responsible for handling network requests and error handling.

- **Managers and Services** - There are many names for those types of classes: "Manager", "Logic", or "Service", but at the end, it's those classes that hold the business logic and act as a wrapper for other APIs such as UserDefaults or Keychain.

169

   – **Database Layer** – Similar to the Network Layer, the
      Database layer is usually a singleton, whether it's based
      on CoreData or SQLite.

There are more examples for Model classes, but the rule thumb is, basically, if it doesn't interact with the user or the UI, it's probably part of the Model layer.

The View – V

The view layer contains all the objects that you see on the user screen and objects that support them. Among the examples are classes that are subclasses of UIView like UIButton, UITableView, and more. But not only are views part of this layer – you can also find transitions, Core Graphics code, animation, layouts, images, and colors.

Importantly, the View doesn't contain any business logic or interacts with the model layer. It doesn't mean View classes are dumb – they are not. There are examples of very sophisticated views, such as MKMapView, UICollectionView, and UITableView. But Views are not familiar with the logic of the data and the app and theoretically can be transferred to other apps without special modifications.

The Controller – C

You already know by now that the Controller is responsible for connecting the view and the model layers. When we're talking about "Controller" in iOS apps, we usually mean "UIViewController".

The UIViewController is the layer that connects the UI and the Model, and this is why UIViewController usually represents a screen in the app and has its own life cycle.

Controller can be any class that connects UI to Model, not just UIViewController. For example, you can connect a progress bar to an audio player class with a controller. The progress bar doesn't know anything about the audio player, and the audio player doesn't know anything about the UI it needs to update. But the Controller wires them together.

Note   The root view inside the UIViewController is not part of the "Controller" layer. It is considered to be part of the View layer; therefore it also doesn't need to be aware of the "Model."

The Problem with MVC

One of the pitfalls MVC has is that it can lead to other MVC form – **Massive View Controller**.

UIViewControllers can become huge – they might contain business logic, persistent data saving, response to user actions, life cycle code, and more. But the biggest problem of all is that MVC pattern is hard to test.

Remember, most of the things we the developers do in mobile development revolve around UI and responding to the UI actions. UI elements are hard to use in tests – there's a life cycle you need to mock somehow, XIB loading, and layout issues. The line between logic and UI is blurred – this is how MVP/MVVM design patterns were created.

MVP/MVVM

We know what a Model is, and we know what a View is. I want to focus now on the term **Controller**. As I said before, the Controller is the glue that manages the data flow between the Model and the View. But in iOS, the Controller is part of the UI – it contains the root view, it has IBOutlets and

IBActions, and it is part of the Storyboard. And since the Controller (may I say now **UIView**Controller) is part of the UI, we can cautiously say it is part of the **View** layer.

What is the "real" controller? MVP and MVVM are two design patterns that share roughly the same principles and are here to solve this question.

In MVVM, we can find another layer called **View-Model**. In MVP, we can find this layer with another name – **Presenter**. In both patterns, the UIViewController (our old "controller") becomes part of the View layer when the Presenter/View-Model becomes the Controller layer. The main difference between the Presenter and the View-Model is its implementation.

Look at Figures 6-4 (MVP) and 6-5 (MVVM).

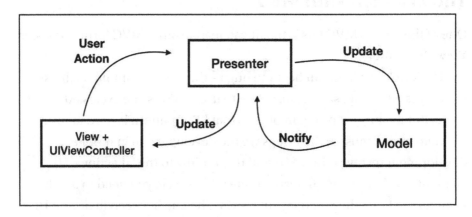

Figure 6-4. *MVP design pattern*

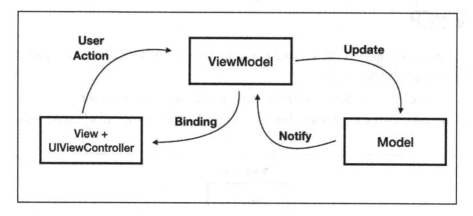

Figure 6-5. *MVVM design pattern*

As you can see in Figures 6-4 and 6-5, MVP and MVVM are not only similar to each other but are also the MVC design pattern.

What is the difference between MVP/MVVM and MVC? Well, just like the classic Controller in MVC, the Presenter and the ViewModel are connected to the View and Model and are responsible of the updates and data flows between the layers. The Presenter and the ViewModel are clean from any UI elements, which makes them much easier to test and maintain.

As I said, the main difference between MVVM and MVP is their implementation.

In MVP, the Presenter **has a reference to the View** (actually, the UIViewController) in the form of a protocol. In MVVM, the ViewModel doesn't have any reference to the View, and the data flow is based on **data binding**, meaning you can use KVO, closures, or reactive programming frameworks like RxSwift or ReactiveCocoa.

The use of MVVM/MVP helps us uphold the principle **of separation of concerns** better. The UIViewController contains so much UI logic, and moving it to the View part makes so much more sense in this case. If you want to make your app more testable, choosing MVVM/MVP over MVC is a good move.

VIPER

For most people, VIPER is a snake. But in this case, VIPER is an upgraded version of MVVM/MVP.

While MVP/MVVM has three components, VIPER has two more components – the Router and Interactor. Let's look at how it looks (Figure 6-6).

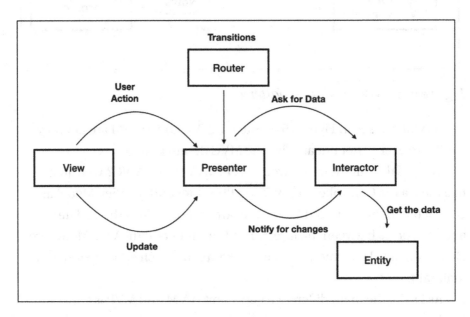

Figure 6-6. *VIPER design pattern*

OK, we need to understand what's going on here:

- We have the View and the Presenter just like MVP.

- For getting the data, the Presenter asks a component called **Interactor**.

- The Interactor goes to the business logic and asks for the data. This business logic is the **Entity** part of the pattern. The Interactor receives back the data and notifies the Presenter with the change.

- The Presenter updates the UI with the new data for the Interactor.

- The **Router** part is responsible for transitioning the user to this screen.

VIPER is considered to be a better design pattern for testing and scale because it fulfills the separation of concern with five different components. Before you run and refactor your code to VIPER, I want to highlight some notes here:

- VIPER should be a **protocol-based** architecture, meaning all the interaction between all components needs to be through a protocol only and not directly. This can be very helpful in testing, but not only that – the protocol actually defines what the rules and the data flow in your architecture are, and in such modular pattern, this issue is much more critical.

- I want to explain the **Interactor** part because it has an important job here. First, it needs to **convert the data** it receives (the Entity) to a readable format the presenter and the UI can understand and work with. The Interactor should be the only component that "knows" the entity and interacts with it. Another task the Interactor has is to **work with business logic and system services**. This can help you mock your presenter easily and simulate many situations you can't simulate in any other way.

- VIPER can be an **overkill** for simple screens and features. Try to adapt the design pattern to the feature you build.

Comparison Between Different Design Patterns

Remember, there isn't "The Best Design Pattern." All have cons and pros, and you should know the differences to choose the right one for you.

Table 6-1 can help you make the right decision.

Table 6-1. *General Comparison Between the Design Patterns*

	MVC	MVP	MVVM	VIPER
Distribution of responsibilities	Problematic	Better	Better	Best
Ease of use	Easy	Easy	Can be hard	Hard
Testability	Problematic	Better	Better	Best

As you can see, VIPER is the best pattern in terms of testing, while MVC is easier for development. Quality isn't just testing; it's also simple, and not all your features/screens need to be with the same architecture. Choose the one that is suitable for your needs.

Summary

Writing a better designed code is a crucial step to do before you start testing your app. The main goal of the chapter is to get you to the position where you can mock different components or easily test different functions. Remember, it is more important to follow the principles described here and not just copy the implementation you see here or in other places.

Next - tests are not only based on code but also on UI. This is what the next chapter is all about.

CHAPTER 7

User Interface Tests

I don't care if it works on your machine! We are not shipping your machine!

—Vidiu Platon

Introduction

Going back to the beginning of the book, I mentioned the Testing Pyramid. If you recall, UI tests are considered to be pricey and less cost-effective than Integration Tests, not to mention Unit Tests.

Nevertheless, it doesn't mean you should avoid UI Tests altogether. UI Tests can be beneficial in many flows – from basic sanity through performance tests and user flows in specific screens.

In this chapter, you will learn

- How UI Test works and how it is different from unit and integration tests

- How to write a basic UI Test

- How to interact with elements on the screen

- How to deal with issues in UI Tests

- What is "Page Object Model" and how it can help you maintain your tests over time

- How to read your test reports, improve their readability, and attach relevant contextual data

- Take advantage of more features of UI Tests such as multi-app testing and dragging

Adding UI Tests

Adding UI Tests is easy and is similar to adding unit tests. If your project doesn't contain the UI Test bundle already, you can go to File ➤ New ➤ Target... and choose the UI Testing template from the popup window (Figure 7-1). You can use the search field to locate it quickly.

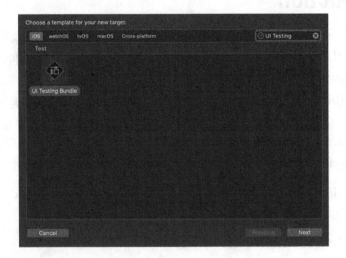

Figure 7-1. *Adding UI Testing target*

The next screen is also similar to adding a unit test target screen (Figure 7-2).

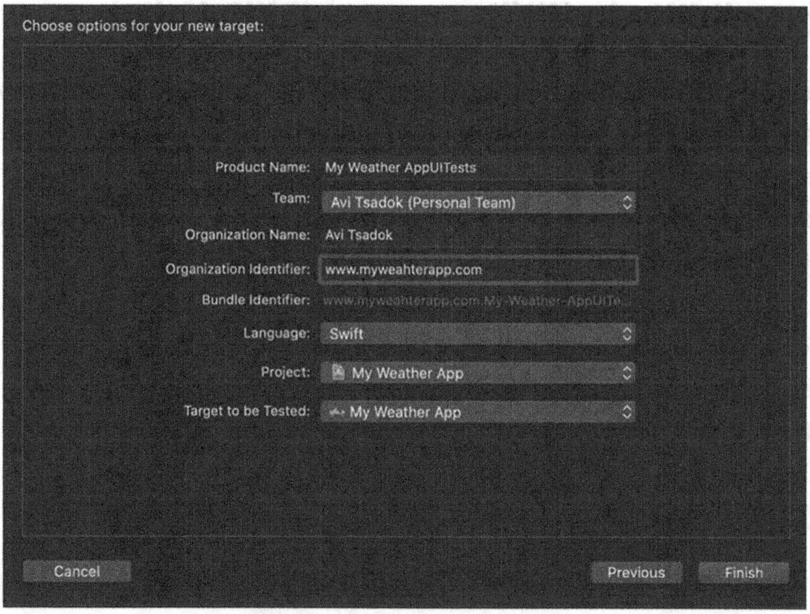

Figure 7-2. *Options window for the new UI testing target*

The new target we create contains one test case, besides the regular info.plist file any target contains.

By looking at the new fresh file, you can tell it's quite different than the unit test code you are already familiar with. The changes start at the top of the file when the "@testable import <module name>" line is missing. To understand why, you need to know how UI Tests work.

How Do UI Tests Work?

Xcode refers to your UI Test bundle as a black box, meaning it doesn't have access to your application code at all. When the test runner starts, it creates a temporary outsider app that launches your app and activates it.

To do that, XCTest uses the **Accessibility framework in UIKit**.

Accessibility in UIKit – accessibilityLabel

If you are not familiar with Accessibility in UIKit, UI Testing is a great place to start. Accessibility in UIKit is not something new, and it helps disabled users interact with apps in many ways. Every UIView conforms to a protocol named UIAccessibility that allows iOS features such as VoiceOver to identify the different UI elements on the screen.

One of the main properties included in the UIAccessibility protocol is **accessibilityLabel**, which represents the name of the element on the screen for disabled users.

There are two easy ways of setting an accessibilityLabel. You can do that by code

```
saveButton.accessibilityLabel = "save"
```

or by going to the Identity Inspector pane in your storyboard (Figure 7-3).

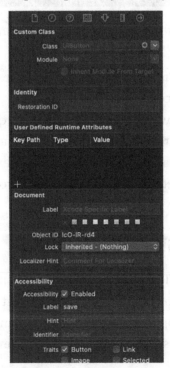

Figure 7-3. *Accessibility Inspector inside the Identity Inspector*

Some controls such as UIButtons have a "built-in" accessibilityLabel which holds the value of their label unless defined otherwise.

When running UI Tests, XCTest uses the accessibility labels to "see" the elements on the screen and, by that, do actions such as tapping, scrolling, typing, and also different validations to make sure the test passed or failed.

Element Tree

Just like the view's hierarchy in your UIWindow, XCTest "sees" this as a tree of accessibility elements.

Take a look at Figure 7-4.

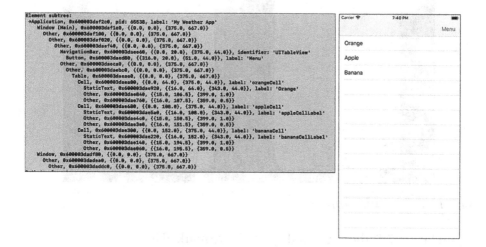

Figure 7-4. *Application screen and its corresponding element tree*

Figure 7-4 displays an app screen and on the left side its element tree, as it was printed in a console. As you can see, we don't have class names or any other "coding" information in the tree – only the types of the elements, their frames, and names. As mentioned before, XCTest looks at our app as a black box and the information available for it.

181

Write Our First UI Test

Let's start with a simple test case. We have a screen with a list of fruits. Tapping on the "Orange" fruit should lead to a new screen. See Figure 7-5.

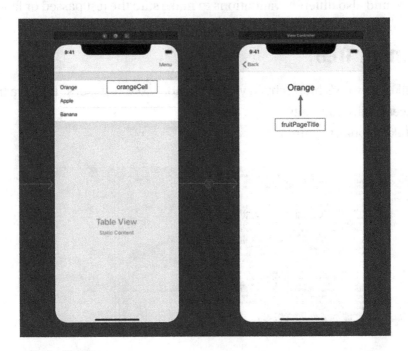

Figure 7-5. *Fruits app*

In Figure 7-5, the accessibility labels are marked in red.

Let's examine our first test code:

```
func testTappingOnOrangeButton() {
        let app = XCUIApplication() //1
    app.launch() //2
    app.cells["orangeCell"].tap() //3

        // assert        XCTAssertTrue(app.staticTexts
                        ["fruitPageTitle"].exists) //4
  }
```

It is surprising how easy it is to set up a short UI Test with not much effort. These are the steps in details:

//1 : Create a reference to **XCUIApplication**, which represents the application you are testing.

//2 : Launch the application.

//3 : Runs query to **find the orange cell** button, and tap on it.

//4 : **Assert** to make sure the next screen appears.

Almost all of your UI Tests start with creating an XCUIApplication instance.

XCUIApplication

XCUIApplication is a proxy for an application. Using this proxy, you can launch an app and get a reference to its visible elements.

The specific application doesn't have to be the application being tested – you can pass bundle identifier on initializing and, by that, running multiple apps' UI Tests:

```
let otherApp = XCUIApplication(bundleIdentifier: "com.myOther
                                                  App.www")
```

Elements

When talking about "elements," we refer to objects that subclass XCUIElement. XCUIElement represents a view on the screen and has properties and methods that let you interact and communicate.

In fact, XCUIApplication itself is a subclass of XCUIElement.

Querying Element(s)

To retrieve elements, we need to query them. Querying is where the accessibilityLabel property comes in hand.

Querying elements are natural. For example, if you want to get the "save" button, all you need to do is

```
app.buttons["save"]
```

The buttons property returns all the buttons on the screen, and the "save" is there to get only the button with an accessibility label named "save".

But what is considered to be a "button"? Is it only controls that subclass from UIButton? Can we create our control and define it as a "button"?

Well, if we return to the Accessibility Inspector in Xcode, we can define the trait for the different views on the screen (Figure 7-6).

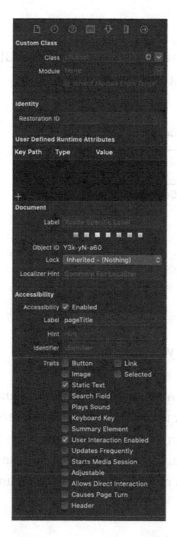

Figure 7-6. *Accessibility Inspector within Identity Inspector, Traits*

Now that we know what traits are available for us and how we can define a trait for an element, let's take a step back and understand how queries for elements work underneath.

How Queries Work?

So, what is the problem with querying elements in UI Testing?

Look at the following diagram (Figure 7-7).

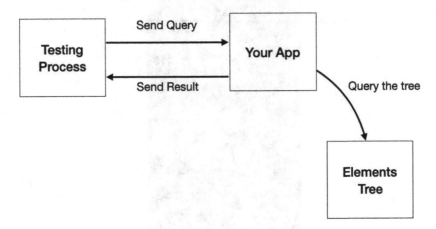

Figure 7-7. *Querying your app for elements*

The querying element mission has some structured pitfalls. First, your app has potentially many elements to go over to retrieve your search results. Also, each element contains many attributes that, in most cases, are not important to your test at all. These pitfalls cause performance and memory issues that may affect your test result and fail it without any justification.

Be Precise with Queries

Let's call back to our last query:

```
app.buttons["save"]
```

Our query has two problems:

- It searches for all buttons on the screen, no matter their position in the view hierarchy.

- It does a full scan on the element tree even after it already found an element named "save".

Those problems lead to potential memory and performance spikes. To easily fix it, we can do a small modification:

```
self.navigationBars.buttons["save"].first
```

We did two crucial changes here – first, we are now searching only in the navigation bar while eliminating the rest of the tree. Second, we used the property "first" to return the first element that we find.

We now understand how to optimize our queries better. But, do you remember I mentioned that, in most cases, we don't need all the element data when querying, but only their references? This leads us to the next optimization.

Resolving Element Data

When querying for a single element, returning its full data is not a big problem. But when querying for a long list of elements, it may cause some memory issues. This is why when querying for elements, they return only as references without their full data:

```
let saveButton = app.navigationBars.buttons["save"].firstMatch
// return only element
let frame = saveButton.frame //resolving the element data
```

XCTest is resolving the element data only when it needs it. So, fetching the button frame is done only when calling the frame property directly using a second query. Similar to what happens in Core Data, if you are familiar with this framework.

Elements by Identifier or Index

Look at the following code:

```
let buttons = app.buttons
```

Unlike you would think, `app.buttons` doesn't return a list of buttons, but a query from the object type XCUIElementQuery. To get the result of the query, it has two important properties:

```
let buttons = app.buttons.
allElementsBoundByAccessibilityElement
let buttons = app.buttons.allElementsBoundByIndex
```

So, what is the difference between these two properties?

Both properties return an array of buttons. The difference is with the resolving method.

We said the querying elements only return their references and not their full data. The complete data fetching is happening later, only by demand. At that point of fetching the data, there's a concern that the actual element tree might have changed.

In this case, XCTest needs to know how to fetch the data on the second query – is it going to be according to its accessibility label or by its index?

We can define it to be by label:

```
let buttons = app.buttons.
allElementsBoundByAccessibilityElement

// changes in the UI....

let firstButton = buttons.first! // fetching its label
```

Or by its index in the array:

```
let buttons = app.buttons.allElementsBoundByIndex

// changes in the UI....

let firstButton = buttons.first! // fetching its index
```

In most cases, we are going to use the first property – fetch them and keep sync with the accessibility label. But there are situations when we don't care about the label but the position of the array, for example, cells of UITableView or UICollectionView.

Examples for Element's Queries

It is always better to be updated with changes in XCTest in that area, since UI Testing evolved by Apple every Xcode version.

But here are some examples to give you an idea of how it works.

To get just get an element by type (if you have multiple elements from this type/trait, you might get an unexpected behavior):

```
app.alerts.element
app.buttons.element
app.collectionViews.element
app.images.element
app.maps.element
app.navigationBars.element
app.pickers.element
app.progressIndicators.element
app.scrollViews.element
app.segmentedControls.element
app.staticTexts.element
app.switches.element
app.tabBars.element
app.tables.element
app.textFields.element
app.textViews.element
app.webViews.element
```

To get an element by its accessibility identifier:

```
app.testFields["password"]
```

To get all images in a specific scroll view (directly):

```
app.scrollViews["Main"].children(matching: .image)
```

To get all the descendant images for the scroll view (including subviews and their subviews, etc.):

```
app.scrollViews["Main"].descendants(matching: .image)
```

To get the fifth element in a query:

```
app.switches.element(bound: 4)
```

Actions on Elements

Getting a reference to an element is useless if we don't interact with it. To simulate the user's actions, we need to have the ability to type, tap, scroll, and swipe on elements.

Fortunately, each XCUIElement has a series of actions you can use that can help you write scripts for your tests quickly.

Note   I recommend you to be updated with Apple Online Documentation with additional available actions.

Table 7-1. *XCUIElement Actions List*

Method Name	Description
typeText(string)	Types a string into an input field element such as text field or text view. Note: The text field needs to be in focus when doing that.
tap()	Taps on a hittable point in the element.
doubleTap()	Sends a double-tap event to the element. Triggers the doubleTap gesture action if it exists.
press(forDuration : TimeInterval)	Is a long touching gesture with a specific duration.
press(forDuration: TimeInterval, thenDragTo: XCUIElement)	Simulates drag and drop event.
twoFingerTap()	Simulates two fingers tap on a hittable element.
tap(withNumberOfTaps: Int, numberOfTouches: Int)	Gives you great flexibility in tapping.
swipeLeft() swipeRight() swipeDown() swipeUp()	Sends a swipe gesture. This is also the way to simulate a scroll.
pinch(withScale: CGFloat, velocity: CGFloat)	Pinches the elements to scale at a specific velocity.

(continued)

Method Name	Description
`adjust(toNormalizedSlider Poisition: CGFloat)`	Is relevant only to UISlider controls – change the value of the slider with a normalized value from 0 to 1. You can use `normalizedSliderPosition: CGFloat` to determine the current slider value.
`adjust(toPickereWheelValue: String)`	Is relevant only to pickers such as UIPickerView and UIDatePickerView.

Here are some examples of interacting with elements:

```
app.buttons["green"].doubleTap() // double tap the green button
```

```
app.textFields["email"].tap() //makes the email textfield the
first responder
```

As you can see, XCTest is full of XCUIElement actions to help you set up (almost) any scenario with your app.

Note   When running UI Tests on the simulator, it is better to make sure the software keyboard is available. Go to I/O ➤ Keyboard and make sure "Connect Hardware Keyboard" is not marked. Simulating a hardware keyboard can cause issues with text fields and text views.

Waiting for Elements

XCUIElements have a simple property called "exists". You can use this property to check if an element is visible on the screen:

```
Let messageExists = app.staticTexts["welcomeMessage"].exists
```

But, UI Tests are not like standard unit tests, in a sense that when you think of it, they actually a-sync tests. Almost every move to a new screen is followed by animation, and many actions such as scrolling or heavy task take time.

When pressing on a button on a page that navigates to a second page, we need to wait for the appearance of the second page before we can do any query for new elements to continue our test.

Instead of writing a "delay" function to halt the program, we have a great function called waitForExistence(timeout:).

waitForExistence(:) halts the execution and waits for the existence of an element before it continues. You can pass a timeout value to make sure the waiting doesn't last forever.

Look at the following code:

```
app.buttons["nextPage"].tap() //navigating to a new page

app.cells["newYork"].waitForExistence(timeout: 1)
app.cells["newYork"].tap()
```

- The user presses on "nextPage" button, and the app navigates to a new screen.

- We wait 1 second for the appearance of a cell called "newYork" on the new screen.

- We press on the cell called "newYork".

"Waiting for elements" plays a lead role in UI Tests and also leads us to the next section – assertions.

Assertions

When talking about assertions in UI Test, it usually means we want to verify the state of the screen. Here are some examples of this kind of verification:

- We want to make sure an element is visible on the screen.

- We want to verify the text or colors on a specific element.

- We want to check the position of an element.

Remember UI Tests are actually a black box, and therefore, you do not have access to the code, just like the user or the tester.

To verify the existence of an element, you can use the waitForExistence(timeout:) function I mentioned earlier:

```
XCTAssertTrue(app.staticTexts["hello"].firstMatch.
waitForExistence(timeout: 2.0))
```

Or text:

```
XCTAssertEqual(app.staticTexts["result"].firstMatch.label)
```

The assertion function we use for unit and integration tests is the same for UI Testing.

Wrap It All Together

We already know how to query elements, interact with them, and assert them. Let's try to pack everything together:

```
func testLogin() throws {
    let app = XCUIApplication()
    app.launch()
    app.textFields["email"].firstMatch.tap()
```

```
app.textFields["email"].firstMatch.
typeText("myEmail@gmail.com")

app.textFields["password"].firstMatch.tap()
app.textFields["password"].firstMatch.
typeText("123456") // It's a bad password. don't
really use it :)
app.buttons["go"].firstMatch.tap()

XCTAssertTrue(app.staticTexts["welcome"].
waitForExistence(timeout: 2.0))
```
}

Great, we wrote our first UI Test!

Let's describe in short what our test does –

it types email and password values in the corresponding text fields, presses on the "go" button, waits for 2 seconds, and then verifies that the welcome message appears.

Notice we had to tap the text fields before inserting the texts, just like a real user.

Record Your Actions

Writing your tests is not the only way to create UI tests. Starting iOS 9, Xcode has a neat feature that lets you record your actions on the simulator and convert them to scripting code in your XCTestCase.

To start recording, locate your cursor inside a UI test method. Once you do that, you will be able to see a record button at the bottom of the Xcode window (Figure 7-8).

Figure 7-8. The record button in Xcode

Clicking the record button again stops the recording.

Notice that the generated code might not be readable and straightforward, like the code you would write yourself.

For example, this is a generated code for typing inside a text field:

```
func testLoginProcess() {

    let app = XCUIApplication()
    app.launch()
    app.textFields["email"].tap()

    let aKey = app.keys["m"]
    aKey.tap()

    let vKey = app.keys["y"]
    vKey.tap()

    let iKey = app.keys["e"]
    iKey.tap()
}
```

And this is just for typing three letters.

But recording your tests can also be useful – sometimes it is hard to do something just by code, like swiping, scrolling, or doing an action with many interactions. Also, it's a great way to discover more possibilities we have in UI Testing.

Dealing with Problems

Not only UI Tests take time to run, but they also require significant efforts to maintain.

There are all kinds of issues with UI Tests:

- Most UI Tests involve **dealing with a server or a network**. Every hiccup in our connection can lead to a test failure.

- The nature of mobile apps is to **change their UI** now and then. While most unit and integration tests can survive UI changes, this is not the case with UI Testing when it is dependent solely on the element tree.

- Also, if you **implement A/B** testing in your app, things may start being messy when the UI is unpredictable.

- Each test has to start with a predictable state. Since the order of the tests is inconsistent (and shouldn't be), you need to reset your state before each test. The problem is you don't have access to your code.

- There are external changes and interactions in the app that are hard to control. A good example is system alerts – for push notifications, location permissions, and more. Those alerts interrupt your test and have an influence on your element tree.

But just like (almost) anything in coding, it is possible to find a decent solution for every problem.

Keeping Your Tests Consistent

The first problem with edge-to-edge tests is that they are dependent on external states such as network and server.

Also, working with a server means that you cannot expect the same response for the same request.

But, if you go back to the Integration Tests chapter, you can see we can simulate the network quickly and make sure we are getting the same responses all the time while eliminating any server or network issues.

The second mission that we have is to make sure we always begin from the same app state. Most of the times, it means

- Cleared User Defaults.

- Cache folder is empty.

- Local persistent store is empty.

- Any temporary files should be cleared.

In general, it means to reset your app when starting a new test case. Just like in previous chapters, we can use launch arguments for that.

To launch your app with specific arguments, you can use the launchArguments property:

```
let app = XCUIApplication()
app.launchArguments = ["-clearDB", "-clearUserDefaults"]
app.launch()
```

And in your app delegate:

```
if CommandLine.arguments.contains("-clearDB") {
        // clear your db
}
```

Launch arguments are perhaps the only way you have to "inject code" to your application in UI Testing. Be careful not to add too many arguments – after all, we want our test to reflect the real-life situation of the app.

Handling System Alerts

As mentioned before, system alerts such as push notification or location permissions can block your test run from interacting with UI elements and by that fail your test.

Sometimes you can synchronize your alerts timing and try to tap the "Allow" button yourself, but I doubt it can be a long-term solution.

So, meet addUIInterruptionMonitor() function. This function is part of XCTestCase, and it can help you monitor and react to any system alerts that your app gets on the way.

Let's see an example for that:

```
addUIInterruptionMonitor(withDescription: "Some System Alert")
{ (alert) -> Bool in
    alert.buttons["Allow"].tap()
    return true
}
```

When calling this function, you need to pass a closure that runs each time your test run detects some interruption. The closure parameter is the XCUIElement that interrupts your test. In most cases, it will be some kind of "alert" element. Querying for the "Allow" button and tapping is a good option to continue with the test.

But what about other alerts? How can you tell what alert is shown? Well, the XCUIElement is just like any other element. Query for its label to find the exact text shown on the screen and by that decide on what button you want to tap.

If you don't know in advance if it's "OK" or "Allow", you can check it:

```
let okButton = alert.buttons["OK"]
if okButton.exists {
  okButton.tap()
}
```

```
let allowButton = alert.buttons["Allow"]
if allowButton.exists {
  allowButton.tap()
 }
```

Or, you can just tap on the "second button"

```
alert.buttons.element(boundBy: 1)
```

Remember that the closure invoked only when there is a system alert. In terms of code, you should continue with writing the test as if the alert never showed.

Note   Dealing with alerts is an excellent example of what is the right approach in UI Tests. These are not standard developer testing, because it's from the point of view of the user. System alerts block the screen for the test runner just like they do for the user, and the handling should be the same.

Sometimes you need to use `waitForExistence` when tapping on one of the alert buttons because there is a delay between the closure invocation and the actual dialog appearance on the screen.

Page Object Model
The Problem

OK, here's a situation – we created several UI tests, and they work great. But after a few weeks, they all started to fail. We did everything according to the book – we handled the system alerts and A/B testing, mocked the network, and cleared everything correctly.

So, what happened?

Well, it seems that we made a change – we added a new step to the login process, and naturally, we now need to update all our tests to the new flow.

As you can see, we have a complicated situation here. We did a small change, and now we need to go over every test and update it. Undoubtedly, it now hurts our motivation to write more UI tests when we know we need to work hard to maintain them. The more UI tests we write, the harder we need to work in the future.

But we have a solution, and it's called the **Page Object Model**.

What Is a Page Object Model?

The idea behind the Page Object Model (or in short POM) is to **separate the test script from the UI locators** and actions. Sometimes, it also means separating the test script from the assertions as well.

For every screen of the app, we create an object that has several types of methods and properties:

- It has methods that **perform main actions**. For example, a method like doSignIn(withEmail email : String, password : String) fills the email text field and the password and starts the sign-in process. It doesn't matter if you do a full refactor on the sign-in screen – the only change you need to do is within the page object.

- It has methods that **check different states**, for example, a method that verifies that you are on the correct screen (isCurrentPageisSignup()) or method that returns a specific value (getWelcomeMessageText()). This eliminates any direct access to the elements themselves and prevents code duplications.

- It has private properties that return central elements on the screen. These are actually **locators** that help us reduce code complications and also make it more transparent.

When we start working with the POM pattern, our test scripts don't have any direct access to the element tree. All the actions are done through the page object.

Another thing, whenever we call the page object for an action that navigates us to a new screen, the page object should return the new screen page object.

Let's take a look at an example for such a page object:

```
class SignInPageObject {

    var app : XCUIApplication

    init(app : XCUIApplication) {
        self.app = app
    }

    private var emailField : XCUIElement {
        return app.textFields["email"].firstMatch
    }

    private var passwordField : XCUIElement {
        return app.textFields["password"].firstMatch
    }

    private var loginButton : XCUIElement {
        return app.buttons["login"].firstMatch
    }

    func doSignIn(withEmail email : String, password : String)-
    >UpsellPageObject {
        emailField.tap()
```

```
    emailField.typeText(email)

    passwordField.tap()
    passwordField.typeText(password)

    loginButton.tap()

    return UpsellPageObject(app: app)
  }
}
```

Here are a few notes about the preceding code:

- We can see the page object **receives the XCUIApplication** in its init() method. This is because the XCUIApplication object is the root object for every UI Test action that we do. You would think that initializing a new XCUIApplication each time can be a good option but take into account that sometimes we initialize XCUIApplication with a specific bundle identifier, so passing on the application object is being on the safe side.

- We have **several private properties** that return the main elements on the screen using simple queries. This is the only place where you query those elements, and whenever the page object needs to interact with those elements, it does it using these properties. The reason they are private is to make sure that we can only access them through the actions and not directly.

- doSignIn() method is doing a standard logging flow, and it's the only non-private method/property we currently have in our page object model. Notice that this method returns our next page object model, UpsellPageObject, which represents the next screen.

203

Now, let's take a look on a code snippet using our page object in test:

```
func testSignIn() {
    let app = XCUIApplication()
    app.launch()

    SignInPageObject(app: app).doSignIn(withEmail: "user",
    password: "12345").pressSkip().verifyWeAreOnTheMainScreen()
}
```

Do you see how simple it is? We can chain our screens to create a concise, readable test and also maintainable.

We call doSignIn(), receive a new object back, press the skip button, obtain a new object back, and verify we are on the right screen – all that with one row. Look at Figure 7-9.

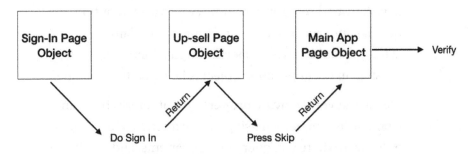

Figure 7-9. *Chaining page objects together*

If you want to get serious about UI Testing in your project, working with POM is not a recommendation – it's a must. Also, this means that recording your tests is only suitable for generating the code. Afterward, you need to take the generated code and organize it in models.

Test Reports

At the end of your test run, the natural thing to do is to read your **test report**. Xcode generates a detailed test report for every run, including test duration and attachments.

The report is generated automatically and can be found in the **Reporter Pane** in Xcode (see Figure 7-10).

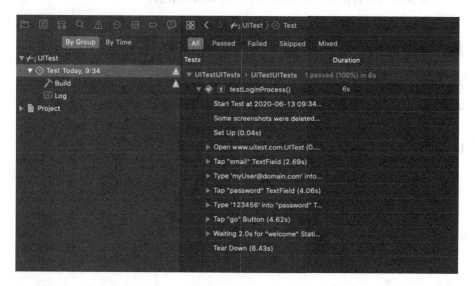

Figure 7-10. *Xcode test report*

Looking at the test report in Figure 7-10 reveals several information details:

- It is possible to filter the tests according to their state. You can see only passed, failed, skipped, or all tests. This is a handful when you have many tests, and you want to focus on the failed ones, for example.

- You can also see how much time each test took. Don't forget that UI Tests take time. This is an opportunity to nail down long-running tests and try to optimize them to reduce the total test duration.

– Also, you can see each small step in your test and how much time it took.

Long-running tests are usually loaded with many steps, and you can find yourself struggling with information overload, trying to find your path.

The solution is to break your test into **activities**.

Activities

Activities are a group of steps you create in UI Tests that are meaningful and can make your test reports look much simpler and short.

Grouping of steps with Activity is very simple. If I want to group my login test script, I will do something like this:

– Step 1 – Enter user email.

– Step 2 – Enter the user password.

– Step 3 – Tap on "Go" button.

– Step 4 – Verify the welcome message.

And to the code, now with activities:

```
func testLoginProcess() {

    let app = XCUIApplication()
    app.launch()

    XCTContext.runActivity(named: "Enter Email") { _ in
        app.textFields["email"].firstMatch.tap()
        app.textFields["email"].firstMatch.
        typeText("myUser@domain.com")
    }
```

```
XCTContext.runActivity(named: "Enter Password") { _ in
    app.textFields["password"].firstMatch.tap()
    app.textFields["password"].firstMatch.
    typeText("123456")
}

XCTContext.runActivity(named: "Pressing Go") { _ in
    app.buttons["go"].firstMatch.tap()
}

XCTContext.runActivity(named: "Verify Welcome Message")
{ _ in
    app.staticTexts["welcome"].firstMatch.
    waitForExistence(timeout: 2.0)
}
}
```

Grouping your steps to activities changes the way your test report looks (Figure 7-11).

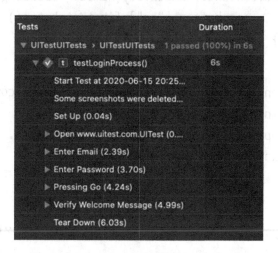

Figure 7-11. *Test report with activities*

Not only that, but you can also group several groups to a new activity:

```
func testLoginProcess() {

    let app = XCUIApplication()
    app.launch()

    XCTContext.runActivity(named: "Do Sign In") { _ in
        XCTContext.runActivity(named: "Enter Email") { _ in
            app.textFields["email"].firstMatch.tap()
            app.textFields["email"].firstMatch.
            typeText("myUser@domain.com")
        }

        XCTContext.runActivity(named: "Enter Password") { _ in
            app.textFields["password"].firstMatch.tap()
            app.textFields["password"].firstMatch.
            typeText("123456")
        }

        XCTContext.runActivity(named: "Pressing Go") { _ in
            app.buttons["go"].firstMatch.tap()
        }
    }

    XCTContext.runActivity(named: "Verify Welcome Message")
    { _ in
        app.staticTexts["welcome"].firstMatch.
        waitForExistence(timeout: 2.0)
    }
}
```

And now, your test report looks even better (Figure 7-12).

Figure 7-12. *Group of activities in a test report*

If you are working with a page object model, it is even easier to implement activities by wrapping the actions with XCTContext. runActivity closure:

```
func doSignIn(withEmail email : String, password : String)-
>UpsellPageObject {
        XCTContext.runActivity(named: "Do Sign In") {_ in
            emailField.tap()
            emailField.typeText(email)

            passwordField.tap()
            passwordField.typeText(password)

            loginButton.tap()
    }

        return UpsellPageObject(app: app)
    }
```

The Page Object Model and Activities go hand in hand. Hooking them together can brighten up your test reports without much effort.

Attachments

One of the most challenging tasks when debugging UI Tests (or actually, debugging in general) is to get information about the state of our app at the time of failure or the state of the app in a particular step that precedes to the failure itself.

Starting Xcode 9.0, Apple added a new feature – XCTAttachment. XCTAttachment gives you the ability to attach useful information to your test report and helps you investigate your failures. But attachments really shine when dealing with a continuous integration environment, for example, not from your computer.

Attachments show up in your test report and can hold different types of data:

- Screenshots

- Images

- Files

- Texts

- Data (blob)

The most common data is, of course, screenshots.

Screenshots

Creating screenshot attachments is a great way to record your test steps to help you diagnose your test failures. Xcode creates screenshots automatically anytime one of your tests fails, but you can also create your own screenshots whenever you want.

To create a screenshot, you need to do three things:

1) Take a screenshot of your screen or one of your elements.

2) Create an attachment based on the snapshot.

3) Add the attachment to the test run.

Here is a quick code snippet to show you how it's done:

```
let screenshot = app.windows.firstMatch.screenshot()
let attachment = XCTAttachment(screenshot: screenshot)
add(attachment)
```

Screenshots in Test Report

The best place to see your screenshots is your test report.

But adding the preceding code to your test probably won't show you any attachment in your test report. Let's take a look at your test report after adding an attachment (Figure 7-13).

Figure 7-13. *Screenshots removed from the test report*

Because screenshots can quickly fill up your storage, we have places where we can handle the lifetime of our attachments.

The first place is the scheme configuration (Figure 7-14).

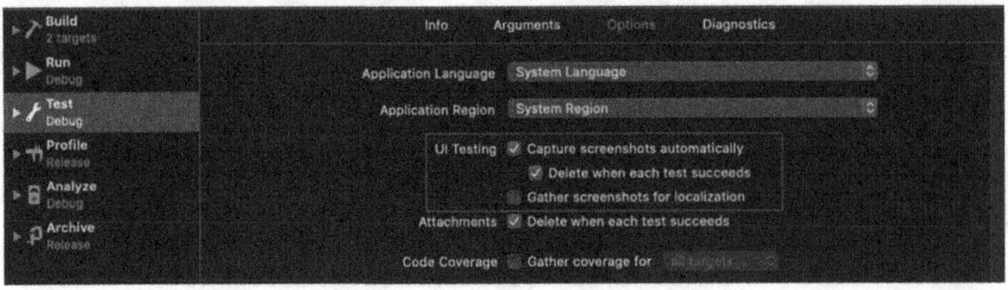

Figure 7-14. *Scheme configuration*

By default, XCTest captures screenshots for every step in your test. This is extremely useful when you want to reproduce your test step by step. XCTest also deletes those screenshots whenever your tests succeed. This option is enabled by default as well.

The second place you can control the lifetime of your attachments is in the code itself:

```
let screenshot = app.screenshot()
let attachment = XCTAttachment(screenshot: screenshot)
attachment.lifetime = .keepAlways
add(attachment)
```

Each attachment has a `lifetime` property, which has two options: `keepAlways` and `deleteOnSuccess`. The default value is `deleteOnSuccess`.

Setting it to `keepAlways` overrides the scheme settings and will keep your attachments regardless of your test results.

Examine Your Attachments

After we changed our scheme configuration or modified our code, we can have a look at our test report to examine our test details (Figure 7-15).

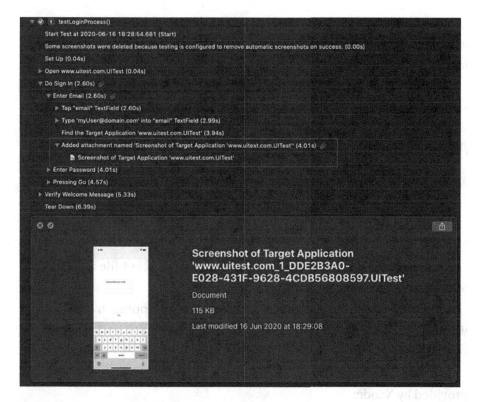

Figure 7-15. *Screenshot in the test report*

If you add attachment inside a specific activity, you will see it under the activity group. Otherwise, it will appear in the root of your test.

Location of Your Screenshots

Many developers run their tests not on a local machine but in a continuous integration environment.

Therefore, they do not have access to Xcode, especially to the Report Navigation pane.

In this case, we need access to the screenshot's files.

Up until Xcode 11, it was easy to access the attachments – they were located in a folder named "Attachments" in the project's derived data folder.

But in Xcode 11, Apple made significant changes in the test results' file structure, and now it's much more complicated to analyze the test results.

About XCResult

Xcode saves each one of your test reports to a file with a type of "XCResult".

Those files are located in the derived data folder under Logs/Test/:

```
~/Library/Developer/Xcode/DerivedData/<Project>/Logs/Test/
```

XCResult file is a package, containing a general .plist file and a data folder with a bunch of binary files.

You can open the XCResult file in Xcode just by tapping it. But if you want to parse it, you may encounter some difficulties and can be cumbersome.

To parse XCResult file, you need to use the provided xcresulttool tool provided by Xcode:

```
xcrun xcresulttool get --path <path of file> --format json
```

Running this command doesn't extract your attachments, but it gives you some general details about your test run.

At this point, you need to locate your test within the JSON and run this command on the specific test by its id:

```
 xcrun xcresulttool get --path <path of file> --format json --id
<testID>
```

On some point, you'll see the attachments section you were waiting for. Then you need to run the export command:

```
xcrun xcresulttool export –path <path of file> --output-path
<Destination path> --id <test id>
```

As you can see, it's not that easy to export attachments from the XCResult file. One option to overcome it is to write your own script to do it easily. Another option can be using an open source command tool that is doing just that. For example, XCParse (`https://github.com/ChargePoint/xcparse`) is a tool that can extract those attachments with only one command:

```
xcparse -s <xcresult file path> <destination path>
```

More Attachment Types

There are additional types of attachments rather than screenshots. For example, you can attach files, strings, audio, and more.

These are the types of available attachments you can create:

- Images

- Screenshots

- Data blob

- Zip archive

- Texts

Let's take a look at how we can create a simple text attachment:

```
let stringAttachment = XCTAttachment(string: "Email:
                    \(emailEntered)")
stringAttachment.lifetime = .keepAlways
add(stringAttachment)
```

And this is how it looks in your test report (Figure 7-16).

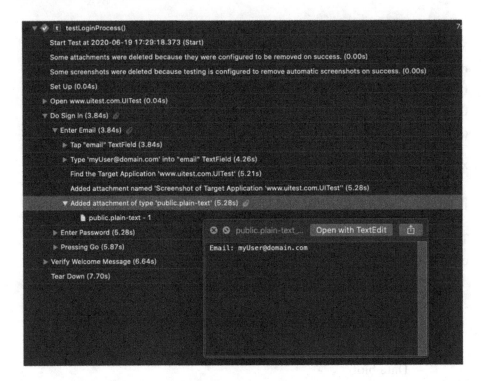

Figure 7-16. *Text attachment in the test report*

You should think about attachments as your way to log your test and leave small pieces of information that can help you investigate your test failures.

More Great UI Test Features

Xcode UI Testing framework has more features and capabilities if you have additional needs. For example, it can help you test your Siri integration, check how your app interacts with other installed apps, and make an advanced dragging gesture.

Testing Your Siri Integration

If your app has a Siri integration, you can start your test with launching it using a Siri phrase:

```
XCUIDevice.shared.siriService.activate(voiceRecognitionText:
"Open My Weather")
```

If you have a Siri intent, you can verify it like we've learned earlier in this chapter – querying your screen elements and asserting them.

Note   For Siri intents, I recommend you use unit testing. There is no point in testing the UI of something that is entirely logical.

Multiple App Testing

If you recall at the beginning of the chapter, I mentioned it is possible to initialize your XCUIApplication object with a specific bundle identifier. If you have multiple apps and you want to test them together, this is an excellent way of doing that:

```
func testMultipleAppsIntegration() {
        let todoApp = XCUIApplication(bundleIdentifier:
        "com.myTodoApp.www")
        let notesApp = XCUIApplication(bundleIdentifier:
        "com.myNotesApp.www")

        todoApp.launch()
        todoApp.buttons["seeMyNotesButton"].tap()

        notesApp.activate()
        notesApp.buttons["addNewNoteButton"].tap()
```

```
            _ = notesApp.textViews["notesTextView"].
            waitForExistence(timeout: 0.5)
    notesApp.textViews["notesTextView"].tap()
    notesApp.textViews["notesTextView"].typeText("This is
    my note")
    notesApp.buttons["saveNewNote"].tap()

    todoApp.activate()
    // check that the new note appears in todo app as well
}
```

What you do need to be aware of is that now you have a new method called activate(). Unlike launch(), activate() doesn't terminate the current running app, but lets you open another app while keeping the existing app alive.

Note   The "Springboard" (the main screen of iOS where you have all your apps) is also an app you can activate with the bundle identifier "com.apple.springboard". Try it!

Dragging Using XCUICoordinate

It is possible to simulate almost any finger movement you want by using something called XCUICoordinate.

XCUICoordinate is an object that represents a location on the screen relative to a specific element. This element can be even the app itself (XCUIApplication object).

After you have a coordinate, you can press it and "drag" it to another coordinate.

For example, here is a code snippet demonstrating how to do a "pull to refresh" easily:

```
func testPullToRefresh() {
        let app = XCUIApplication()
        let fromCoordinate = app.coordinate(withNormalizedOffs
        et: CGVector(dx: 0, dy: 10))
        let toCoordinate = app.coordinate(withNormalizedOffset:
        CGVector(dx: 0, dy: 20))
        fromCoordinate.press(forDuration: 0, thenDragTo:
        toCoordinate)
    }
```

The chances are that you are not going to need it for most of your use cases, but for the ones that you need, it can be convenient.

Summary

UI Tests are harder to maintain for many reasons. But they are great for many tasks as well, sanity checks, for example. They can also be an excellent alternative to integration tests. My recommendation to you is to implement UI testing in your critical flows and cover them.

Another thing UI Tests are useful for is performance tests. We'll discuss performance tests in detail in the next chapter.

CHAPTER 8

Cover Another Aspect of Your App – Performance Testing

Just as athletes can't win without a sophisticated mixture of strategy, form, attitude, tactics, and speed, performance engineering requires a good collection of metrics and tools to deliver the desired business results.

—Todd DeCapua

Introduction

Performance Tests are another aspect of software testing. We can say that performance tests are not about "if things work" but rather "how things work," and that positions them as a unique test bundle compared to the other test methods.

© Avi Tsadok 2020
A. Tsadok, *Pro iOS Testing*, https://doi.org/10.1007/978-1-4842-6382-2_8

In this chapter, you will learn

- What is the basic idea of performance testing

- How `measure()` function works and how to define a baseline

- The different metrics you can use starting from Xcode 11

- How to configure your tests

- How to write a-sync performance testing

- Where Xcode saves your test baseline information so you can adjust it to your CI/CD environment

The Basic Idea of Performance Test

Unlike other tests such as Unit or Integration tests, Performance Tests are a little "catchy." They have several unique characteristics, which make them less predictable.

For example, running performance tests on an old device probably produces different results than running them on a new one.

Also, on one run, you can have a certain result, which may be different than the second or the third run. Not to mention other factors such as machine state, CPU load, free memory, caching, and more.

So, based on the given details, we understand that performance tests work a little bit differently:

- Each tested code runs **several times** to prevent any one-time result that may affect our test results. At the end of the test run, the final results will be based on the **average** of all executions.

- Because the average result might be different from tests to test, it is not enough to satisfy our needs. We still need to set some **baseline** to make sure the change is not too big and it's within the reasonable spectrum.

- The last issue is also a major one – **the baseline is linked to a specific device** based on its UUID. The reason is obvious – not only that each device has different hardware, but it also has different settings and installed software.

So, the unpredictable nature of performance tests makes it a unique creature in our testing suite, and we should use it for specific use cases or flows that may cause us performance issues in future changes.

The Basic Measuring Function

Let's start with writing our first performance test:

```
class PerformanceTests: XCTestCase {

    func testPerformance() {
        let imageProcessor = ImageProcessor()
        measure {
            _ = imageProcessor.generateImage()
        }
    }
}
```

In the preceding test, we have a class named ImageProcessor with a function called generateImage(). We know that the function generateImage() is doing some heavy task, and we want to execute this code as part of the measure function.

223

The Measure() function is part of XCTestCase, and it's the basic performance method we have. It has one single parameter, which is a closure. What measure() function does is executing the closure ten times and calculating the average time in the end.

Let's run the test (Figure 8-1).

```
class PerformanceTests: XCTestCase {

    func testPerformance() {
        let imageProcessor = ImageProcessor()
        measure {
            = imageProcessor.generateImage()      ◇  No baseline average for Time.        ×
        }                                             Time: 1.127 sec
    }
}
```

Figure 8-1. *Running our first performance test*

We see some interesting information after our first run. First, we see the average time, 1.127 seconds. We also see a message saying there is no baseline time. This leads to our third insight – you can see that our test actually passed.

Unlike other tests, performance tests don't use assertion. Instead, we define a **baseline** for our metric to make sure our result stays below it.

Define the Baseline

You don't have to work hard to set a baseline for your test. Pressing on the gray diamond next to the message "No baseline average for Time" opens a small popup window with more details and functionality (see Figure 8-2).

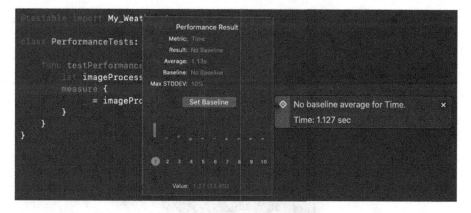

Figure 8-2. *Performance Result Settings window*

In this popup, you can see additional information about your run and an option to set a baseline easily by just pressing a button.

On the lower part of the popup, you can see your executions over time.

Note   It's not rare for the first execution to be much longer than the others. It has to do with things like caching or internal behaviors of the Swift language. This is part of the reason we run this test several times to get a score that is closed to a real-life state.

Pressing the "Set Baseline" button changes the state of the popup window to Edit mode (see Figure 8-3).

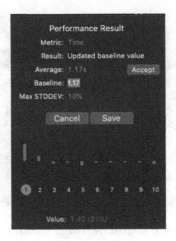

Figure 8-3. Performance test baseline edit

Tapping the "Accept" button sets the current average result as our baseline for the next test.

You can also edit the baseline manually just by tapping it and type the new value.

To confirm the change, just press on "Save".

What the "Baseline" Means for Our Test?

Performance tests are based on two important values – Baseline and Max STDDEV.

The Baseline value is the bar your test needs to reach. If your execution code runs 10%+ slower than the baseline, your test will fail.

Another value being calculated is the standard deviation, the STDDEV. If the deviation of your runs is more than 10%, a value that can be changed easily, your test will fail as well.

Why Is the Deviation Important?

When running performance tests, we need to make sure our score is reliable. If you get a high deviation in your tests, it might be a code smell and point on two things:

- It may be an indication of a problem in your code. Basically, you need to expect heavily loaded code to perform similarly in multiple runs. If this is not the case, it means **your code executes in an unexpected manner** and maybe be affected by external values or states.

- A big deviation means that there **are some executions that are slow**, much slower than the average score you get. It also means that our average score is not relevant and our users experience poor performance even though our test might be below the baseline.

If your test fails because of high deviation, don't increase the bar for no reason. You should investigate the behavior of your code before making any changes.

measure(metrics:) Function

Up until Xcode 11, the only metric you could measure is execution time. But the new Xcode version brought new metrics to the table:

- `XCTClockMetric` – This is the execution time metric similar to what we've learned in the previous section.

- `XCTCPUMetric` – This metric gives you information about the CPU activity during the run.

- `XCTMemoryMetric` – Measure allocated during the test.

- XCTStorageMetric – Record bytes written to disk.

- XCTOSSignpostMetric – Measure execution time for a specific part of your code, defined externally in your code using os_signpost functions.

The most basic metric developers use is the time/clock metric, but there are many cases why you would want to check other metrics as well.

It doesn't mean you need to run the performance test for each one of your metrics – you can pass array of metrics and get results for all of them:

```
func testGeneratingImageWithAllMetrics() {
    let imageProcessor = ImageProcessor()
    measure(metrics: [XCTClockMetric(), XCTCPUMetric(),
    XCTStorageMetric(), XCTMemoryMetric()]) {

        _ = imageProcessor.generateImage()
    }
}
```

Running the test while passing all the metrics gives you the same popup as before, but now with information for each of your metrics (see Figure 8-4).

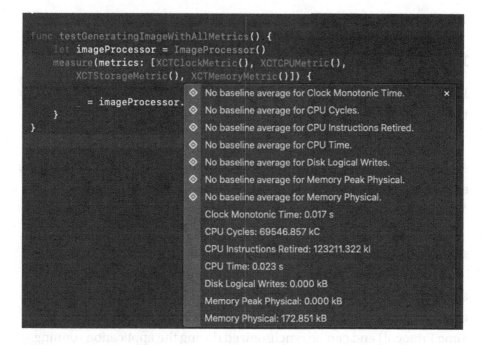

Figure 8-4. *Setting baselines to all metrics*

This is plenty of information! Let's try to dig in and understand what it means.

Analyzing the Metrics

Clock Monotonic Time

This measurement is part of the XCTClockMetric, and it measures the exact duration of your execution block. At this point, I want to explain what exactly **Monotonic Time** means.

If you want to measure code without using the measure function, you can do something like this:

```
let startTime = Date()
_ = imageProcessor.generateImage()
let endTime = Date()
```

```
let duration = startTime.timeIntervalSince1970 - endTime.
timeIntervalSince1970
```

We measure the time before the execution and the time after the execution. Obviously, the elapsed time between them is the duration of the execution, right?

Well, not exactly. Doing that would be wrong.

There are two different clocks in almost every modern operating system – the **Wall Clock** and **Monotonic Clock**.

The **Wall Clock** is the clock that is presented to the user (and the application). This is the time that we get when we use the `Date()` function to get the current time. Wall Clock time is affected by NTP (Network Time Protocol) and can be synchronized during the application running. Therefore, not only the elapsed time might not be accurate; it can even be negative.

Monotonic Clock, on the other hand, cannot be affected by any external influence. Monotonic Clock is not aiming to give the current time since it doesn't have a "starting point." What it does is to give you a stable duration measurement, and this is why we use it in performance tests.

CPU Cycles, CPU Time, and CPU Instructions

OK, so we have a clock time, why do we need a "CPU Time"? And what is it anyway?

So, first, **CPU Time** doesn't represent the total execution time, but only the time the CPU was busy executing your instructions. For example, the total execution duration also includes any I/O operations or even network requests (although it's not recommended to include network time in your performance tests).

So, if you want to eliminate any external factors and focus on your processing time, CPU Time under XCTCPUMetric is the way to go.

So, what are **CPU Instructions Retired and CPU cycles?**

CPU Cycles is the metric that shows you how much your CPU worked hard during the block execution, and CPU Instructions metric contains the number of the actual instructions completed – in general, a low number of instructions for the same task, points of better efficiency, and power consumption.

Checking Your Writing Activity with XCTStorageMetric

XCTStorageMetric is another interesting aspect of the performance tests. Instead of measuring time, it measures your writing to disk activity. This might not sound like an interesting metric, but when concluding it with the clock metric, it's a great metric to help you optimize your code.

Writing to disk is considered to be a heavy task much more than writing to memory. It is best practice to avoid it if possible. A big increase in this metric can explain poor results in the clock metric and can be an indication of unnecessary writing activity.

More Configuration with XCTMeasureOptions

Using performance metrics is pretty straightforward. In fact, they are so useful and effective that you don't really need any configuration for them. But, still, there is an option that can help you tune your performance tests better to get more accurate results.

The way of doing that is bypassing an object of type XCTMeasureOptions. XCTMeasureOptions was added along with the performance test metrics, and it has two properties that you are able to configure.

iterationCount

The first property you can update is the `iterationCount`. This property defines the number of times your test runs. The default is 5, but you should be aware that XCTest always adds another iteration and ignores it (it actually ignores the first one).

Why would we want to change the number of iterations? There could be two reasons – the first one is **heavy and time-consuming** performance tests that you want to run no more than one or two times. The second option might be the opposite – very small performance tests that you need to run many times to get accurate results as possible.

In 95% of the cases, you don't need to change the default value. Also, if you run your test without passing an `XCTMeasureOptions` object, the number of iterations will be ten times and not five as described earlier in this chapter.

invocationOptions

Performance tests are great, but they still have one major drawback, and that's controlling the start and the end of the measured part of your code.

I'll explain – we know that performance tests run multiple times, and they all should start from the **same state**. In fact, they are exactly like any other tests – you need to have some setup code before you start and do a cleanup when you finish.

The problem is that you need to execute the setup and cleanup code **inside the** measured block, which means that all the metrics cover these parts of your block as well.

The `invocationOptions` property lets you define how your measurements are taken. It's an optionSet that has two options – `manuallyStart` and `manuallyStop`.

If invocationOptions contains manuallyStart, it means that measurements are taken when you call the function self. startMeasure() in your execution code. If manuallyStop is included in invocationOptions, it means the Xcode stops the measurement when on self.stopMeasure().

Look at the following code:

```
func testGeneratingImageWithAllMetrics() {
    let imageProcessor = ImageProcessor()
    let options = XCTMeasureOptions()
    options.invocationOptions = [.manuallyStop ,.manuallyStart]
    measure(metrics: [XCTClockMetric(), XCTCPUMetric(),
    XCTStorageMetric(), XCTMemoryMetric()], options:
    options) {

        // do some preparations

        self.startMeasuring()

        _ = imageProcessor.generateImage()

        self.stopMeasuring()

        // do some cleanup
    }
}
```

Looking at the code, you can see we can easily insert some setup and cleanup code inside our execution closure and define exactly what part we want to measure.

Measuring App Launch

One great way you can make use of performance tests is to measure your app launch.

App launch time is extremely important to your app user experience and, in many cases, is the root of ongoing frustrations among users.

Setting up a test for that mission is very easy. In fact, you don't need to do anything – any new UI testing target comes with a predefined app launch test:

```
func testLaunchPerformance() throws {
    if #available(macOS 10.15, iOS 13.0, tvOS 13.0, *) {
        // This measures how long it takes to launch your
        application.
        measure(metrics: [XCTOSSignpostMetric.
        applicationLaunch]) {
            XCUIApplication().launch()
        }
    }
}
```

It is pretty amazing that in two rows we can measure our app launch time.

This test also contains baseline just like all the other performance tests, and since it's already written for you, it's recommended for you to include it in your test bundle.

Asynchronous Performance Tests

So, we can see how easy it is to measure the performance of a specific function/method by just wrapping it inside the measuring closure. But what if we want to measure an a-sync function?

In general, it is much simpler to measure synced functions, but it is still possible to also test a-sync function using the XCTestExpectation tool we've learned in previous chapters.

Note   If you don't remember how to use XCTestExpectation, go back to the unit test chapters and go over this part.

The basic steps to create a performance test for a-sync function are as follows:

- Open measuring closure while setting the automaticallyStart to yes.

- Create the XCTestExpectations **inside** the closure. Now, this step is important. Creating the expectation object outside the closure will raise an exception.

- Wait for the expectation to be fulfilled inside the closure, just like the expectation's creation itself.

Let's see an example:

```
func testImagePrcessongAsync() {
    measure(metrics: [XCTClockMetric()]) {
        let expectation = XCTestExpectation(description: "Image
        processing")
        let imageProcessing = ImageProcessor()
        imageProcessing.generateImageAsync {
            expectation.fulfill()
        }

        wait(for: [expectation], timeout: 2.0)
    }
}
```

Remember that executions run one after the other, so the `wait()` function halts the run until the expectation is fulfilled before it continues to the next one.

Also, you need to be careful about the waiting timeout duration – if it's too low, say, lower than the baseline, the test can fail even though it ran better than the baseline.

The Baseline Under the Hood

Unlike other tests, performance tests rely on the specs of the machine that runs them.

So, you can conclude that different machines give you different results; therefore, the baseline has to be corresponding to the host machine.

And this is something you need to understand, especially if you run your tests on a continuous integration environment – Xcode saves the baseline values for any combination of the host machine (your Mac) and device (including simulators).

Although iOS simulators are not emulators, meaning there shouldn't be any CPU difference, they can still give you different results.

For example, you might turn off/on different features for different devices in your code. Also, the device resolution can have an impact on the simulator performance (again, this is up to the host machine as well).

Where Xcode Saves the Baseline?

This is an important question, especially if you work in a big corporate, and your app integration process is running on different machines.

True to Xcode 12, the baseline values are saved inside your Xcode project file.

Xcode project file (*.xcodeproj) is a package, meaning it's actually a folder that displayed like a typical file.

To reveal the package content, right-click the package (xcodeproj) and select "**Show Package Contents**".

Navigate to xcshareddata/xcbaselines/.

The first important file you see there is info.plist. This file contains the list of the "host machine+device" combinations. Xcode generates a unique UUID for each combination and saves it (see Figure 8-5).

***Figure 8-5.** Info.plist file, containing the host machine details along with the target device information*

If you look at the info.plist, you'll see the generated UUID. For each UUID, Xcode creates **another** plist file in the same directory, containing the list of baselines for each test method (Figure 8-6).

Key	Type	Value
▼ Root	Dictionary	(1 item)
▼ classNames	Dictionary	(1 item)
▼ PerformanceTests	Dictionary	(2 items)
▼ testGeneratingImageWithAllMetrics()	Dictionary	(2 items)
▼ com.apple.dt.XCTMetric_CPU.cycles	Dictionary	(2 items)
baselineAverage	Number	51,700
baselineIntegrationDisplayName	String	Local Baseline
▶ com.apple.dt.XCTMetric_CPU.instructions_retired	Dictionary	(2 items)

Figure 8-6. *List of test methods and their baselines for each metric*

How Xcode Pulls the Baseline from These Files

If you take a look again at Figure 8-5, you can see that Xcode doesn't save the serial number of the machine, but rather its specs. This means that if you run your tests on a different machine but with the same specs, Xcode will pull the corresponding baselines for this test.

Why is this important? Because this is the way you can set the baselines for your CI environment – by adjusting the "combo" settings to match your remote machine.

Summary

You don't have to write performance tests for every method in your project. More than that, there are projects that performance tests are useless.

Performance is all about the big numbers – if you have heavily loaded functions or pieces of code, this tool is a great way to optimize them and verify you don't have any regressions. Not only testing performance on small, unimportant function is useless; it's also a mistake that can make the maintenance of your test difficult.

We are heading to the next chapter – a technique that can help you define the "expected result" easily.

CHAPTER 9

Snapshot Testing

Reminds me of the awesome bug report I saw once: 'Everything is broken. Steps to reproduce: do anything. Expected result: it should work.'

—Felipe Knorr Kuhn

Introduction

When we think about writing tests, we usually think about defining expected results and then writing tests to validate them. But what if we know our code already executes as expected, and all we want to do is to prevent regression in the future?

Snapshot testing is all about saving our current state persistency once we know it's stable and then making an ongoing comparison in each run.

In this chapter, you will learn

- What is Snapshot Testing

- How to write your own snapshot testing

- What are the problems with snapshot testing

- What are UI Snapshot Testing and why do we need it

- Meeting FBSnapshotTestCase as an example for a UI Snapshot Testing Framework

© Avi Tsadok 2020
A. Tsadok, *Pro iOS Testing*, https://doi.org/10.1007/978-1-4842-6382-2_9

What Is Snapshot Testing?

The following diagram (Figure 9-1) is the best way to explain what a snapshot testing is.

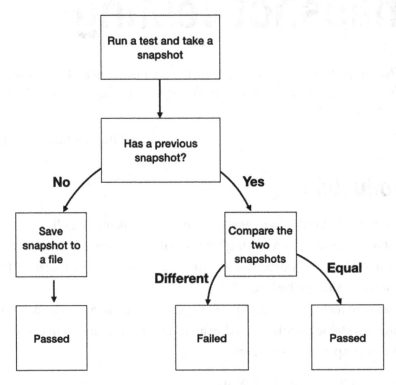

Figure 9-1. *What is a snapshot testing*

Snapshot testing is a technique that can help you write tests quickly and easily in cases it's too complicated to cover it with the regular unit or integration tests. For example, snapshot testing is a great way to cover UI elements of your app or network responses.

This technique is not recommended in all cases. Still, before I explain why we should be careful not to become addicted to snapshot testing, I want to dive into the practice – how snapshot testing works.

Snapshot Testing from Scratch

Let's say we have a function that receives a sentence (as a string) and return its verb.

This is the function signature:

```
func getSentenceComponents(sentence : String)->Components?
```

Now let's write our first test for this function:

```
func testExtractComponents() {
    // arrange
    let str = "The man is running"

    // act
    let verb = SentencesAnalyzer().getVerb(sentence: str)!
    let reference = ""

    // assert
    XCTAssertEqual(verb, reference)
}
```

If you pay attention to the preceding code, you can see we did something new here – we created an empty string called reference and compared it to the result of the function. Now, we know the test is going to fail because the preceding sentence has a verb – "running."

After running the test, we receive the expected failure message:

```
XCTAssertEqual failed: ("running") is not equal to ("")
```

Even though our test failed, **we know** our code works as expected. So, all we need to do now is fix our test, and set "running" as the value of reference:

```
func testExtractComponents() {
    // arrange
    let str = "The man is running"

    // act
    let verb = SentencesAnalyzer().getVerb(sentence: str)!
    let reference = "running"

    // assert
    XCTAssertEqual(verb, reference)
}
```

That was our first snapshot testing!

Let's summarize it:

- We wrote a test when we compare the result to an empty string.

- We ran the test, took the result of the function, and saved it to the reference variable.

- We reran the test and see that it passes.

So, the first run is only to get the expected result, and every test from now on takes a "snapshot" of the current state and compares it to the saved result from earlier.

Using Swift Keywords

If we want to complete the process of saving snapshot to a file, we need to understand the challenges we have here.

First, we need to save all the snapshots to a file, so we'll have access to them when we run our tests. To get a directory relative to our test target, we can use the #file keyword. If you recall, we've learned about swift keywords in the Unit Testing chapter, and #file is another keyword we can use here.

#file returns the absolute path for the current file:

```
let snapshotTestingDirectory = URL(fileURLWithPath: "\(#file)")
        .deletingPathExtension()
```

The preceding code returns a directory with the name of the testing file, but without the .swift extension. It's a neat trick to quickly produce a relative directory to the file you are working on.

Now that we have our snapshot folder, we need to save a snapshot for each function. Swift keyword feature comes to rescue once again with #function. #function returns the name of the current function, and this can be the keyword to our snapshot database.

We can save a snapshot file for each function, or we can keep all snapshots in a big JSON file inside our snapshot's directory.

Let's create a path for our snapshot file based on the function name:

```
let snapShotFileForFunction = snapshotTestingDirectory.appendin
gPathComponent(#function).appendingPathExtension("snapshot")
```

Let's continue the code with creating the folder and saving/reading the snapshot and see the full code:

```
func testExtractComponents() {
    // arrange
    let str = "The man is running"

    // act
    let verb = SentencesAnalyzer().getVerb(sentence: str)!

    let snapshotTestingDirectory = URL(fileURLWithPath:
    "\(#file)")
    .deletingPathExtension()
```

```
let snapShotFileForFunction = snapshotTestingDirectory.appe
ndingPathComponent(#function).appendingPathExtension
("snapshot")

let fileManager = FileManager.default
try! fileManager.createDirectory(at: snapshotTestingDirecto
ry,withIntermediateDirectories: true)

if fileManager.fileExists(atPath: snapShotFileForFunction.
path) {
  let reference =
    try! String(contentsOf: snapShotFileForFunction,
    encoding: .utf8)
  XCTAssertEqual(reference, verb)
} else {
  try! verb.write(to: snapShotFileForFunction, atomically:
  true, encoding: .utf8)
  XCTFail("Failed to write snapshot")
}
}
```

Creating Our Assertion Function

Extracting the code to a function makes it reusable in other tests as well:

```
func doAssertSnapshot(match data : Any) {
      var stringData = ""
      dump(data, to: &stringData)
      let snapshotTestingDirectory = URL(fileURLWithPath:
      "\(#file)")
      .deletingPathExtension()
```

```
let snapShotFileForFunction = snapshotTestingDirectory.
appendingPathComponent(#function).appendingPathExtensio
n("snapshot")

let fileManager = FileManager.default
try! fileManager.createDirectory(at: snapshotTestingDir
ectory,withIntermediateDirectories: true)

if fileManager.fileExists(atPath:
snapShotFileForFunction.path) {
  let reference =
    try! String(contentsOf: snapShotFileForFunction,
    encoding: .utf8)
  XCTAssertEqual(reference, stringData)
} else {
  try! stringData.write(to: snapShotFileForFunction,
  atomically: true, encoding: .utf8)
  XCTFail("Failed to write snapshot")
}
}
```

Notice that we convert the Any object that we get to a string using the dump() swift function.

But we haven't finished quite yet. If you remember, when we discussed about custom assertion, we said that we need to pass the swift keywords such as #file and #line to our custom assertion function. Same goes here – we need to pass #file, #line, and also #function to our new assertion code:

```
func doAssertSnapshot(match data : Any, file : StaticString =
#file, line : UInt = #line, function : String = #function) {
    var stringData = ""
    dump(data, to: &stringData)
```

```
        let snapshotTestingDirectory = URL(fileURLWithPath:
        "\(file)")
        .deletingPathExtension()

        let snapShotFileForFunction = snapshotTestingDirectory.
        appendingPathComponent(function).appendingPathExtension
        ("snapshot")

        let fileManager = FileManager.default
        try! fileManager.createDirectory(at: snapshotTesting
        Directory,withIntermediateDirectories: true)

        if fileManager.fileExists(atPath:
        snapShotFileForFunction.path) {
          let reference =
            try! String(contentsOf: snapShotFileForFunction,
            encoding: .utf8)
            XCTAssertEqual(reference, stringData, file : file,
            line : line)
        } else {
          try! stringData.write(to: snapShotFileForFunction,
          atomically: true, encoding: .utf8)
          XCTFail("Failed to write snapshot", file : file, line :
          line)
        }
    }
```

Now our new test looks like this:

```
func testExtractComponents() {
    // arrange
    let str = "The man is running"

    // act
    let verb = SentencesAnalyzer().getVerb(sentence: str)!
```

```
    // assert
    doAssertSnapshot(match: verb)
}
```

With only one line, we did both assertions and saved the result for the next test.

Snapshot Testing Drawbacks

We can see that with a fair amount of code, we can implement snapshot testing in our bundle quite easily. It doesn't mean that snapshot testing is a perfect solution – it's not. Snapshot testing has its issues, and you need to be familiar with some of them. Let's list some of them.

Documentation Is Missing

In the first chapter, I mentioned that tests are actually our documentation to the code. While defining the expected behavior precisely and in details, lead us to the appropriate state step by step, tests are actually the best documentation you can have for your app.

Some of this documentation, or may I say, the crucial part of it – the expected result - is hidden in a data file instead of being upfront. Sure, we can document it in a comment right within the test, but if we do that, what's the point of snapshot testing?

Too Easy to Fix

When regular unit tests fail as a result of code changes, we need to define the expected result manually. This is a welcome process that forces us to recheck our code and verify if it works as expected. Snapshot testing, on the other hand, makes this process to be "too easy." With a click of a button, we delete the associated file and create a new snapshot.

In general, fixing tests shouldn't be that easy – when you fix a failed snapshot test, it actually means you are doing a **manual test** to verify that the function (or the state) you are testing is working as expected. And we all know what happens when a manual operation is involved in the process – it usually means it's not going to happen.

Why My Tests Failed

Unit tests are usually narrowed. It means that you are checking a specific function with a particular condition. So, when you have a failed test, it is really easy to understand **why** it failed. This is not always the case with snapshot testing. In snapshot testing, we often check a state or a big chunk of serialized data. The nature of snapshot testing makes it hard for us to get to the bottom of the issue.

UI Snapshot Testing with iOSSnapshotTestCase

One of the areas that snapshot testing really shines is UI Snapshot testing.

Unlike data snapshot testing, which can be handled easily using TDD, UI snapshot testing has a real comparative advantage.

Imagine the following scenario – you take screenshots of main screens in your app, and in every test run, you validate they stay the same at the pixel level. This is something that UI designers have trouble to do, not to mention QA testers.

Why Do We Need That?

UI Screens are very vulnerable. Text changes can affect your UI, changes in reusable UI components can break existing screens, and even OS updates can break your UI screens.

Not only that; as mentioned before, sometimes it's hard to notice those changes without making a real diff process.

iOSSnapshotTestCase

Many, many years ago (actually, it's only 5–6 years), Facebook developed an open source framework named FBSnapshotTestCase. After a short period, Facebook ditched this project and created a new internal project. Fortunately, Uber took ownership of maintaining the framework. Now the framework is named iOSSnapshotTestCase, and you can find it here: https://github.com/uber/ios-snapshot-test-case.

How Does It Work?

Once iOSSnapshotTestCase is installed, it is elementary to make use of it in your app. The process is based on two steps:

- Run the test in **record mode**, meaning there is no comparison made, just saving the initial state to the file system.

- Change the record mode to **false,** and then run again to see that there are no changes vs. the saved snapshot.

Each test method initializes a view or a CALayer, comparing it to the current screenshot it has.

The expected screenshots are saved in the file system. Each test case has its own folder, and every test method has its own file with the name of the method.

Set Up and Run iOSSnapshotTestCase

Setting up iOSSnapshotTestCase is easier than you think.

The first step is to install the framework using any popular dependency manager, for instance, CocoaPods.

Install Using CocoaPods

Once CocoaPods is installed (you are more than welcome to search Google for how to install this great dependency manager), it's easy to add iOSSnapshotTestCase to your `Podfile`:

```
target 'MyWeatherAppTests' do
  inherit! :search_paths
  # Pods for testing
  pod 'iOSSnapshotTestCase'
end
```

Remember to add the framework to your test target and not your primary target.

Defining Environment Variables

The second step is to configure the environment variables. These variables define the folders where our snapshots are saved. It is best practice to set the values recommended by the documentation:

```
FB_REFERENCE_IMAGE_DIR = $(SOURCE_ROOT)/$(PROJECT_NAME)Tests/
Snapshots/ReferenceImages
```

```
IMAGE_DIFF_DIR = $(SOURCE_ROOT)$/(PROJECT_NAME)Tests/Snapshots/
FailureDiffs
```

If you remember, environment variables are set in the scheme editor (Figure 9-2).

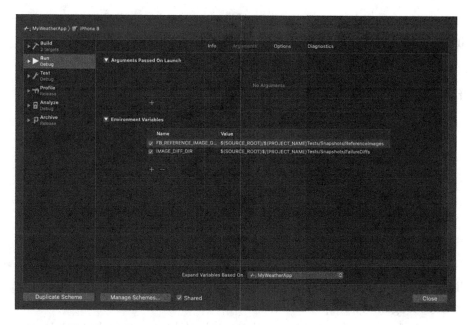

Figure 9-2. *Scheme editor*

Notice the format – it adds "Tests" right after the project name. That's because the default target name for unit tests is the project name followed by the word "Tests". You just need to make sure that's the case in your project.

Subclass FBSnapshotTestCase

Unlike other unit tests, for the snapshot testing to work, you need to subclass FBSnapshotTestCase (which subclasses XCTestCase).

FBSnapshotTestCase handles all the snapshot testing for you.

The first thing you need to do is to import the FBSnapshotTestCase framework:

```
import FBSnapshotTestCase
```

Again, remember that in your `Podfile` you need to include the snapshot framework under the test target and not under your primary target.

Let's build our first snapshot testing:

```
func testSnapshotMainScreen() {
        // arrange
        let controller = CityWeatherViewController(nibName:
        "CityWeatherViewController", bundle: nil)

        // assert
        FBSnapshotVerifyViewController(controller)
    }
```

Oh, dear, it's that easy! Yes, snapshot testing (in this case) is only two lines. The first line initializes the view controller, and the second line verifies it against a snapshot.

And of course, the problem is that we don't have a snapshot yet. If we run the test as it is, we get an error message (Figure 9-3).

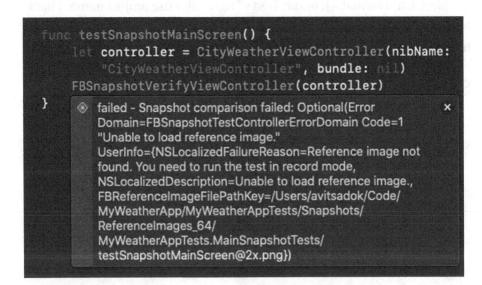

Figure 9-3. Running a snapshot test for the first time

To make sure we have a snapshot for a specific function, we need to run the test in a record mode. To do that, turn on the record mode under the setup() method:

```
override func setUp() {
    super.setUp()
    self.recordMode = true
}
```

"recordMode" goes over the verification functions, and instead of verifying them, it creates a snapshot and saves it in the folder defined in your scheme.

Now, let's run the test with record mode and see what happens (Figure 9-4).

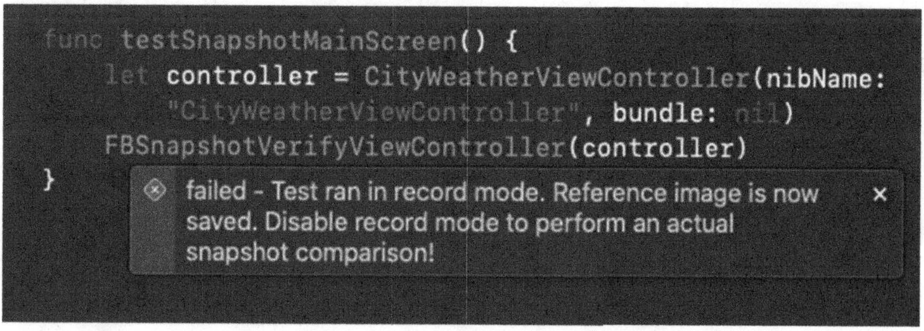

Figure 9-4. *Running a snapshot test in record mode*

Oh no, another error! Don't worry; this is perfectly normal. The reason the test fails is to remind us that we need to disable the record mode to make sure that from now on our test will be verified against a snapshot.

But first, let's make sure a snapshot has been saved in our file system (see Figure 9-5).

Figure 9-5. *The snapshot is saved in our file system*

Now that we have a snapshot, we can disable record mode

```swift
override func setUp() {
    super.setUp()
    self.recordMode = false
}
```

and rerun our test (see Figure 9-6).

```swift
func testSnapshotMainScreen() {
    let controller = CityWeatherViewController(nibName:
        "CityWeatherViewController", bundle: nil)
    FBSnapshotVerifyViewController(controller)
}
```

Figure 9-6. *Running the test when record mode is disabled*

That's it. Now we can verify our screens automatically.

Verification Failure

Let's say that we made some UI re-design in a specific screen in our app by changing the particular font size. What we didn't know is that we broke our CityWeather screen.

Let's see what happens when we run our snapshot test (see Figure 9-7).

```
func testSnapshotMainScreen() {
    let controller = CityWeatherViewController(nibName:
        "                           ", bundle: nil)
    FBSnapshotVerifyViewController(controller)
}
```

⊙ failed - Snapshot comparison failed: Optional(Error   ✕
Domain=FBSnapshotTestControllerErrorDomain Code=4 "Images
different" UserInfo={NSLocalizedFailureReason=image pixels
differed by more than 0.00% from the reference image,
FBDiffedImageKey=<UIImage:0x6000039d55f0 anonymous
{375, 667}>, FBReferenceImageKey=<UIImage:0x6000039d8d80
anonymous {375, 667}>,
FBCapturedImageKey=<UIImage:0x6000039d0ab0 anonymous
{375, 667}>, NSLocalizedDescription=Images different})

Figure 9-7. *Regression in snapshot testing*

The verification function detects the UI has been changed and causes our test to fail.

Now, one of the essential things in tests is the ability to identify the reason for the failure.

Back to the scheme editor, we had to define a variable named "IMAGE_ DIFF_DIR". This is an optional variable that contains the path for the diff folder in case of a failure.

Let's go back now to our file system (Figure 9-8).

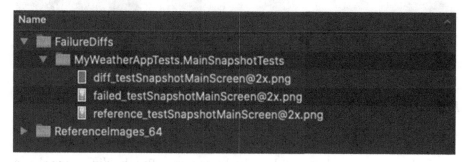

Figure 9-8. *FailureDiffs folder in case of a failure*

We see that we have three images:

- **Reference_**<name_of_test_function> – This is the snap-shot file that was created when we initially ran the test in record mode.

- **Failed_**<name_of_test_function> – This is the latest snapshot that failed. This one is different from the reference UI.

- **Diff__**<name_of_test_function> – This is the most important file here. This is an image that shows only the difference of pixels between the two images.

Let's open the three files (Figure 9-9).

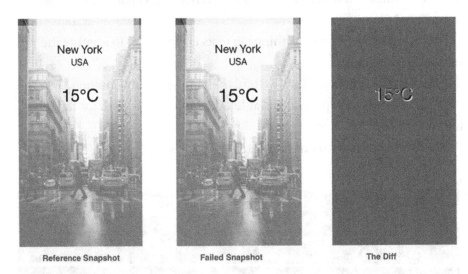

Reference Snapshot   Failed Snapshot   The Diff

Figure 9-9. *The three images FBSnapshotTestCase generated for us*

At first glance, it seems that the reference and the failed snapshot are identical – something that could easily slip our eyes. But the diff image clears things up – we can see that the temperature's font size has increased. The diff image shows **only** that change, so we can directly focus on the change.

Snapshot Testing Configuration

The best thing about snapshot testing is its simplicity – with literally two lines of code, we can create a snapshot test that detects changing our eyes can barely see at first glance.

But it doesn't mean we cannot adjust and tune the test for our needs.

Include Device Information

By default, the generated snapshot file name is composed only out of the test method name, for example:

testSnapshotMainScreen@2x.png

Of course, this means that if we want to check our views on different devices and OS versions, this might be a problem.

Fortunately, the FBSnapshotTestCase class has a property named fileNameOptions, which lets you configure the name of the file:

```
override func setUp() {
    super.setUp()
    self.recordMode = true
    self.fileNameOptions = [.device, .OS ,.screenSize]
}
```

The generated file name, now when running on iPhone 11 simulator with iOS 13, is

testSnapshotMainScreen_iPhone_13_6_414x896.png

Personally, I think this is very handy, especially when testing full-screen views, when there are significant changes with safe area spaces between devices.

Control the Tolerance for Changes and More

In my last example, we see that a small change caused our test to fail. And this might be awesome – those regressions are sometimes hard to catch. The only question is "how much do we care?" We are aware that our changes can cause regressions here and there, but sometimes we want our test to fail, starting from a certain level of difference.

If you need more control over your snapshot testing, you can use the snapshotVerifyViewOrLayer function.

This function has some interesting parameters:

- **viewOrLayer** – You can pass either view (UIView) or a Core Animation Layer (CALayer).

- **Identifier** – Why do we need an identifier? Well, you know our views are usually dynamic, meaning we can configure them to display different data or states. The identifier you give to your snapshot is also added to the snapshot file name. This means you can test your screen/ view in different states and keep a reference image for each state. This may sound optional, but I find this option extremely useful.

- **Suffixes** – Here, you can add a suffix to your test folder.

- **perPixelTolerance** – A float represents the tolerance to changes in the RGB of your pixels. "0" means no change is acceptable, and "1" means every change is acceptable.

- **overallTolerance** – This is the total tolerance for changes (both color and pixel location).

- **defaultReferenceDirectory** – In case you don't define the reference directory in your scheme, you can do it here.

- **defaultImageDiffDirectory** – Same goes here. You can define the diff directory right from your snapshot assertion function.

Let's take a look on how to use it:

```
func testSnapshotMainScreen() {
    let controller = CityWeatherViewController(nibName:
    "CityWeatherViewController", bundle: nil)
    controller.city = "New York"
    let result = snapshotVerifyViewOrLayer(controller.view.
    layer, identifier: "NewYork", suffixes: ["cities"],
    overallTolerance: 0.1, defaultReferenceDirectory: nil,
    defaultImageDiffDirectory: nil)
    XCTAssertEqual(result, "")
}
```

As you can see, the directory parameters are not mandatory, and you can just pass nil in case it's already defined in your scheme.

Summary

Snapshot Testing is a great way to write tests that involve big chunk or serialized data quickly. But it really shines when talking about UI Snapshot Testing.

My recommendation is to take the simple path. It is easy to set up and maintain, but as always, too much of it can cause you big headaches in the future. In fact, some developers ignore snapshot as a principle manner.

Summary

CHAPTER 10

Implement Tests in Our Daily Work Routine

No amount of testing can prove a software right, a single test can prove a software wrong.

—Amir Ghahrai

Introduction

We discussed many types of tests – unit, integration, performance, UI, and snapshot tests. But if you ask me what the most challenging task in writing tests is, I would say actually writing them.

Being a developer is not easy. Our daily schedule is full of stress – deadlines, bugs, documentation to read, meetings, and some of us have an angry boss who sits on our head. Eventually, we are full of excuses for why we don't have time right now for tests.

Writing the right tests, narrowing down the important ones, and deciding what will be the focus, this are another challenges that we, as iOS Developers, have to deal with.

© Avi Tsadok 2020
A. Tsadok, *Pro iOS Testing*, https://doi.org/10.1007/978-1-4842-6382-2_10

In this chapter, you will learn

1. How to write tests as part of your development routine

2. How to build a good mix of unit, integration, and UI tests

3. How to compose test scenarios

4. What is "code coverage" and how to manage it in Xcode

How Do We Start?

So, to solve that, we need to understand the keys that we need to follow.

Tests Are Part of the Development Task

While many developers tend to leave writing tests to the end of the development cycle, this is a crucial mistake. First, in most cases, our development tasks encounter difficulties, and we need to give up on something to finish our feature by time. What is more comfortable than giving up on writing tests? We "know" our app works fine; anyway we have a QA session, and we do have a deadline.

We need to understand that writing tests are an integral part of the development itself. Wrote a complicated function? We write a unit test for her to make sure our code works fine. When we postpone it to the end of the development session, we're, in fact, saying "If everything works out exactly as planned, I'll have time to write tests." Most chances are it's not going to happen.

We Need to Decide What to Test

Don't test everything. Not only getting everything covered is not efficient, but it also costs you more maintenance in the long run. Understand not only the benefit of each test but also **its price**.

Use each test technique (unit, integrations, etc.) for its purpose. If you have a class full of sophisticated code, cover it deeply with unit tests. But if you have something like this

```
func onSaveButtonTapped()  {
    interactor.saveToFile()
}
```

there's no need to cover that with a unit test. Just move on.

Fixed a Bug? Write a Test

This one follows the previous point. We can't tell what our problems will be and what bugs we are going to bump into (otherwise, we would handle them in the first place).

One great technique is to write a test **for every bug we find**. When we have a bug, it is a great indication for a less covered but yet important area of our code. In this case, it is better to use the TDD (Test-Driven Development) approach and write the test **before** we fix the bug.

Test Mix

Now that we understand **when** to write our tests, we need to understand **what** to write. Unit tests are easy to write. Should we write more of them? Or should we go on UI Tests to try to automate the end-user experience?

This is not an easy question. It depends on your team resources, on your project structure, and on even your app business model. But still, there are some methodologies we follow, and we call it Test Pyramids.

The Test Pyramids

Each type of test has different influences on our daily work. For example, UI Tests are pricey. They may check user interaction and sometimes end-to-end scenarios, but they are hard to build and maintain and take a long time to run. Unit tests, on the other hand, run very fast and catch issues closer to the code, but they don't tell anything about your app from the user perspective point, and they cannot test your app flows or even how your parts work together. The strategy where to invest more time and effort is crucial to our work. In his book, *Succeeding with Agile*, Mike Cohn describes this strategy as the "Test Automation Pyramid" or, in short, the "Test Pyramid." The Test Pyramid is a visual way to describe a mixture of test automation suite that balances between development efforts and efficiency.

The Classic Pyramid

What considered to be the best practice and the most famous pyramid is the classic pyramid. The traditional pyramid is the one you probably see when the question of "what is the mix of tests we need to do" appears (see Figure 10-1).

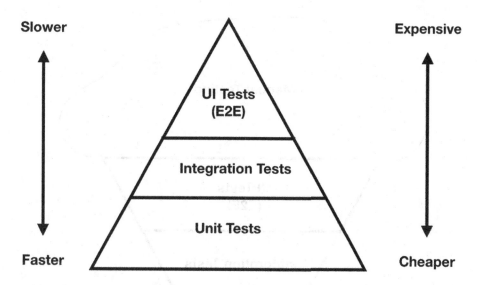

Figure 10-1. *The classic pyramid*

According to the "Classic Test Pyramid," we should write as many unit tests as we can. We should also write integration tests, but less than unit units, and write even less E2E (UI Tests). As mentioned earlier, the idea is to balance between speed and effectiveness. Another reason is that we want to catch the bugs and defects closer to the code at the low level, and this can be done easier with unit tests.

When we're going up in the pyramid, we get away from the code and go closer to the user. Also, since UI and APIs change more often than logic functions, when we're going up in the pyramid, we find ourselves invest more effort in maintaining those layers.

The Ice Cream Cone Model

Considered to be an anti-pattern but acceptable in specific development teams is the **Ice Cream Cone** model. In this model, the pyramid is flipped upside down (Figure 10-2).

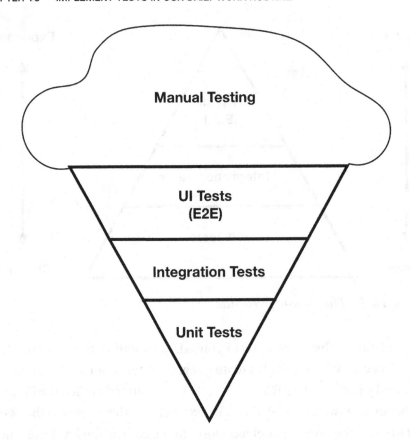

Figure 10-2. *The Ice Cream Cone pattern*

The Ice Cream Cone pattern is getting less and less popular. However, there are still companies that adopt this model, mainly big companies that have resources to maintain this monster or companies that their user flows are simple. Ice Cream Cone model is focusing a lot on GUI and end-to-end testing. In most cases, you can find different teams work on different types of tests without any collaboration or any sync between the development team and the product team.

Since UI Tests cover end-to-end cases, meaning closer to the user, there is an assumption that the more UI Tests we create, the more effective the test suite is.

But there are several problems with this anti-pattern:

- **It's harder to build**. Building a UI Test scenario requires preparation of the UI elements and much time in creating the flows. Also, the verification that your tests run as they should takes a fair amount of time.

- **UI Tests take time to run**. Each test can easily take 10 seconds and even more, depending on the app and the scenario, while unit tests take less than 0.1 seconds in the worst part. Integration test can also take a fair amount of time when running in front of a server or a network. When you run a test suite that contains many UI and integration tests, you take into account that those tests can take 30+ minutes to run, and that can be an issue in a continuous integration environment.

- **It's harder to fix and maintain**. Detecting issues is good, but when you catch a bug far from code, it is harder to fix. When a unit test fails, you get the exact broken method. Also, every change in the UI requires us to modify the UI test as well; otherwise, the long-running suite breaks.

However, there are several techniques to avoid Ice Cream Cone pattern:

- **Collaboration** – Make sure the different teammates (the developers, the QA, and the automation team) are synchronized. Try "Pair Testing", to encourage teammates to be aligned on what we are testing and how. Focus on better "kick-off" meetings to make sure the feature or the mission is clear to everyone.

- **Give Priority to Unit Tests** – Unit tests run fast and easy to maintain. As mentioned earlier, there is a reason why we need to test our app closer to code – closer to the code means more comfortable to fix. Unit tests allow us to focus on a specific piece of code and cover it with all cases, something that it's impossible to do in GUI testing. Also, it's straightforward to write unit tests and run them, so their cost is cheap compared to other tests.

- **Explicit Agreement of the Testing Mix** – Try to define the percentage of tests, which are unit tests, and the percentage of tests that are GUI. The testing mix is something that needs to be clear to all workers and needs to be managed by the team leader. Try to decide exactly what are the critical integrations and user flows you need to cover with tests that are not unit tests and create only them.

The Testing Diamond

So we agree that end-to-end (UI) tests are difficult to create and maintain. They take too much time to run, and they are sensitive to small UI changes. But there is a significant advantage of end-to-end testing – the ability to test your app as a system and not as an isolated piece of code each time.

Some say that the most important tests you can do are to check how your units work together. Although the end-to-end tests fill that need, we do need to balance between their effectiveness to the speed and ease of unit tests. The answer here is Integration tests, which are often considered to be the "forgotten" layer of the test pyramid. The resulting pattern is "Testing Diamond" (Figure 10-3).

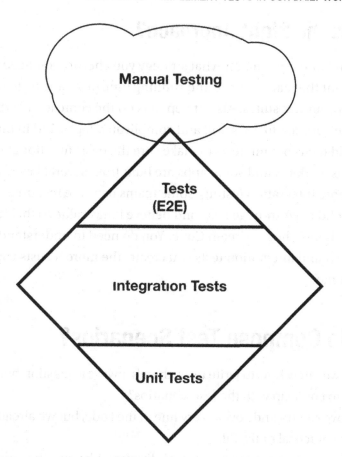

Figure 10-3. *The diamond pattern*

As you can see, the testing diamond is focusing mainly on integration tests based on the belief that most of the business-related issues and scenarios are in this layer. These integrations are between your units. This approach is to look at "the problem" as a complex system that needed to be tested and not just individual units. In general, the testing diamond can give you much higher confidence in your app stability and quality, because it's closer to the business and product requirements than unit tests; however, they are most costly to create.

What Is the Right Approach?

The bottom line is no matter what strategy you choose, you need to take into account the maintenance and running time of your tests to decide the mix of your test suites. Also, it depends on the context and type of app. Some apps are full of small and complicated logic, and in that case, you should focus on unit tests to make sure the basic functionality of your app is working, and some apps are built from several layers and require more integration testing. Some teams have the resources to create a solid edge-to-edge tests and believe it has value to their app so that they choose the Ice Cream Cone. You do need to understand that the more UI and integration tests you create, the more it costs you in terms of time.

How to Compose Test Scenarios?

Now that we know how to write tests, there's always a question bumping up – how to come up with the test scenarios?

Sure, we can try and cover every line in the code, but we already know this is now practical or useful.

There are two approaches I want to discuss with you – the one is **TDD** (Test-Driven Development) and **BDD** (Behavior-Driven Development). As you can tell by their name, both approaches are driven by something. The list of tests driving the TDD and BDD is driven by the product requirements.

You don't have to follow those approaches one by one. But it can give you a direction on how to write tests along with your code.

Test-Driven Development (TDD)

All code is guilty until proven innocent.

Test-Driven Development (TDD) is a software development technique that states a simple principle – write your tests before writing the code. While that sounds simple, it is a big thing for the developer. TDD ensures the developer is aware and knows all the requirements from its class or function, and when done right, it leads to high code coverage and minimum bugs.

Developers consider TDD to be part of something called Extreme Programming; a methodology started to gain momentum in the late 1990s.

Kent Beck, a software developer, developed TDD as a technique, and while it's simple to understand, it requires different thinking on how to approach the code and the functions.

Look at the following diagram (Figure 10-4).

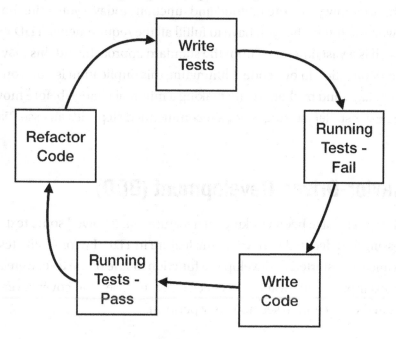

Figure 10-4. TDD life cycle

TDD starts with writing a test that fails on the first run (because we haven't written any code yet). After running the test and seeing that it fails, we write the code that satisfies the requirement and rerun the test to see that it is passing. We refactor our method, verify again with testing, and then repeat the first step by adding a new test and continue with the implementation.

This process makes sure we are adding the minimum code that we need for the function/class to operate correctly.

Let's stop for a minute and talk about the refactor part – some think that, in this case, refactor means "write better code." But when you think of it, it sounds weird – we just wrote this code, so how come we need to refactor it? Well, when doing a test-code-test-code process, we are writing the function or the code block step by step according to the tests, and this is a different approach of writing code than writing the function in one session.

Think of how you write method and functions today – you write the code with the intent that you have to fulfill all the requirements. TDD approach is a vast difference from the standard approach, and this may lead to duplication in our code. Eliminating this duplication is done on the refactor stage, and by that, we are making a minimal change before moving to the next test. Refactoring is not a recommended step – it's an essential step.

Behavior-Driven Development (BDD)

A real story is I have been working on a feature that involved some text processing and decided to develop the feature in TDD. I wrote some tests in advance and started to develop the function. Some of the tests were a list of text inputs, and I wanted to check different cases and cover several points in the function to see how they perform.

So, with test coverage of 100% of the function, I distributed a build to the QA, and after 10–15 minutes of QA testing, the app crashed. I said to myself, "But it was TDD! I covered every single expression in the code!". The QA tester was checking a use case where the user used an emoji character in his input. That caused an exception of out of bounds because of encoding issues.

Based on the bug's history and reviews combined with a pre-thinking process, the QA team decided to check this scenario, and that was the result.

So how come the fantastic process of TDD didn't catch it? That's the result of a situation when a developer works apart from the product and QA teams. Also, TDD aims to cover code, not to answer real-world problems. And this is fine – thinking about possible and common user behaviors is a mission that requires teamwork and collaboration. It's not a technical issue but rather a procedural issue. When teams don't work together, those things happen quite often, and the preceding example is considered to be a light and an easy one. There are use cases that not only affect a specific line in the code but can force you to refactor some of your implementations if you don't think about those cases in advance.

The solution here is to combine BDD (Behavior-Driven Development) to your process. BDD is a collaborative process between the product manager, the QA team, and the developer, which aims to define different use cases from the user perspective, to direct the development, and to focus it on the real-time world scenarios.

The collaboration between the product, the QA, and the development teams can cover many user scenarios and real-world tests. To do this, the team is having a "discovery meeting" where they start writing together user stories when each one of the teammates brings value to the table.

The Product Owner is responsible for converting user stories into features, defining the scope of the product, answering user experience questions, and making sure the solutions brought up are aligned with the feature requirements.

The QA tester brings his experience and knowledge about how users behave and what are the common pitfalls. He also thinks about edge cases and how the application can break. QA can also represent "monkey testing" – what if a monkey is playing with the product, pressing fast on buttons, touching different places on the screen, entering a huge input, and more?

The developer can bring his knowledge about practical solutions and constraints related to what he can do. He is the only one who knows how the app works underneath and adds the technical layer that is so important to the discussion.

The three team heads' mission is to write tests in plain English, in a way that everyone can understand and is answering all the product requirements.

BDD doesn't come instead of TDD, but it helps the TDD process to focus on the crucial tests. You can think of BDD as part of the design process of the feature and TDD as part of the development itself. Some say that the BDD is TDD done right or that it's an extension of TDD. I think that TDD done without BDD is an inefficient process, and it's better to implement BDD in your workflow rather than do a pure TDD without any context.

How to Write Good BDD Scenarios

More than the act of testing, the act of designing tests is one of the best bug preventers known. The thinking that must be done to create a useful test can discover and eliminate bugs before they are coded – indeed, test-design thinking can discover and eliminate bugs at every stage in the creation of software, from conception to specification, to design, coding and the rest.

—Boris Beizer

Take a look at the following scenario:

"Tapping the register button should start the registration
process"

We have several problems writing a test for that scenario. For example, we don't know what fields currently have values. We also assume that the user is on the registration screen, but we only know that because we see there is a register button in the scenario, not because it is mentioned. We may have a register button in different places such as popups or even other screens, so it's important to mention the name of the screen in that case. The last thing is there is no title for this scenario and no number, so it is hard to find it and put it in a database for later use.

Now look at the following scenario:

SCENARIO 01: User Registration from the registration Page GIVEN
the user is on the registration page
AND the following fields are filled:
- Email
- Full Name
- Password
WHEN the user confirm the form
THEN the app should start the registration process

In the preceding example, we describe the context – what is the current screen for the user and on what fields there is an input. We describe the action – "confirm the form" (it can be either the register button or the return button on the keyboard) – and we also describe the expected behavior.

This style of writing is called GHERKO, and it is an acceptable way of writing user scenarios in BDD. Several basic terms are being used here:

GIVEN – This describes the current state of the scenario, for example:

- On what screen the user is? Is he logged in? What do the input fields contain?

- What is the network condition?

- What is currently saved in the DB?

This section includes the minimum details and conditions that are relevant to the scenario.

WHEN – This describes the action the user performs in this scenario. Try to make this part more declarative and less technical to cover multiple tests.

THEN – This is the expected result when the action described is performed. Remember, it is supposed to be something that can be measured somehow so we can automatically test it.

AND – This can be used in GIVEN, WHEN, and THEN sections to describe multiple states, actions, or results. Sometimes, if you have many conditions, you can use a list like in the preceding example.

Those test scenarios are an excellent opportunity for the team to communicate with each other regarding the product and the development process. The QA testers are in charge of writing the scenarios when the developer is in charge of the steps. The product manager is the one that makes sure the scenarios are in the scope, answering the product requirements and that it does not conflict with them in any way. The recommended method is for the developer and the tester to work in pairs.

Some tips for writing scenarios are as follows:

- **Try to write declarative scenarios** to cover as many use cases as you can. In the "WHEN" rows, try to write the intentions and not the actual actions. For example, in the preceding example, the user intends to confirm the form. It doesn't matter if it's by pressing the button or pressing the return key on the keyboard. Writing "Tapping the submit button" is a UX action that is not related to the scenario and can even confuse both the developer and the QA. Also, writing UI actions (such as tapping/swiping) can narrow down the number of tests to only button tapping. Remember, one scenario can produce multiple tests. Remember that sometimes tapping on a specific button can be an important scenario as opposed to pressing a keyboard button, so this rule is not always valid. It depends on the scenario.

- **Use real-world data when writing your scenarios.**
  Those scenarios are not supposed to check edge cases such as very long inputs, a significant amount of data, or low connectivity. Writing real-world data improves the communication between the developer, the QA, and the product manager by making sure everyone understands the situation we are talking about. For example, don't use "1" or "test" as the first name in the form earlier. For a start, it doesn't express what we imagine the text input contains and also when we read the scenario a few days later. It's not clear what we meant when we wrote it.

Many times when writing scenarios, it's really easy to write one that covers multiple areas or check several issues. **Try to focus on one test per scenario**. When your scenario refers to different tests or areas, you can have several problems:

- Multiple tests in the same scenarios mean there are dependencies between them. If the first test fails, the others fail as well, and we want to isolate those tests and not chain them together.

- Look at the following sczenario:

```
SCENARIO 02: User Registration from the registration Page GIVEN
the user is on the registration page
AND the following fields are filled:
- Email
- Full Name
- Password
WHEN the user confirm the form
THEN the app should start the registration process AND
continue to the next screen
```

> - Take a look at the THEN section. It seems that the team
> was a little bit lazy and didn't want to break the scenario
> into two scenarios. They added two expected results – one
> is to start the registration process, and the second one
> continues to the next screen. In this case, we may find two
> different people that work in that area of the app. The first
> one is responsible for building the form, and the second
> developer is responsible for the Server API or with the
> navigation of the app. This situation where multiple
> people are in charge of fixing or testing the same scenario
> is not ideal.

> - **Understand the GHERKO language**, and use it right.
> Here is a lousy example of a scenario written in GHERKO:

```
SCENARIO 03: User Adding A New Note
GIVEN the user opens the app main menu
AND the user navigates to the notes screen WHEN the user tapped
on ADD NOTE button THEN "Add New Screen" opened
WHEN the user types note details
AND her the user tap the "Save Button" THEN screen is closed
```

- Clearly, the writer of the scenario doesn't understand the GHERKO syntax or how to write useful tests. In the preceding example, the GIVEN section describes an action ("The user opens the app main menu") instead of a given state. But the worst part is the WHEN-THEN pair. The order of the commands is always GIVEN-WHEN-THEN, so WHEN cannot appear after THEN. Each WHEN-THEN pair is new behavior, and therefore, you should slice them to two scenarios. Also, that kind of scenario contains duplicates. Imagine we have a document with all the scenarios. Most chances are we already have a scenario that describes what happens when you tap on the ADD NOTE button, so this scenario is already covered. The solution is to use the GIVEN section properly. The GIVEN section should bring the user the desirable state. Take a look at the fixed version of the preceding scenario:

SCENARIO 03: User Adding A New Note GIVEN the user in on the add new screen AND there is text in the input field WHEN the user tap the "Save Button" THEN screen is closed

It's not only better, but it's also shorter and takes less time to read and write.

- Make sure the scenarios are **written in English and not a technical language**, so anyone in the team can understand them, especially the non-tech guys. Don't talk about "flags," file names, queries, and so on. Keep the scenario simple and user wording.

- Since this book covers automated tests, when you write BDD scenarios, keep in mind that those scenarios need to be easily automated, meaning don't write scenarios that are hard to measure, such as "THEN it needs to animated smooth" and so on.

The final step after writing down and agreeing about all the scenarios is for the developer to create tests out of them – some can be unit tests, some integration tests, and some UI Tests. To create tests, your code must be testable (test-friendly); otherwise, writing those tests will be hard at best and impossible at worst.

Code Coverage

Code coverage is a measure used to determine what is the percentage of your code that gets executed during testing. Since UI Tests refer to your app as a black box, code coverage is only relevant for unit tests and integration tests.

To enable code coverage in Xcode, you need to enable it in your scheme configuration, while it is not enabled on default. This action is explained in detail in the next chapter.

Code Coverage calculations are straightforward – if you have ten lines of code and your tests execute seven of them, you have code coverage of 70% (7/10). Many teams try to achieve high coverage based on the assumption that "higher is better."

Don't Set a Target for Code Coverage

Setting a target for code coverage is something developers tend to do – assuming that high code coverage means high-quality code. I'm afraid that's not right. It's not that high code coverage is terrible – it isn't, and it can tell you many things about your code, but the last thing it tells you is your code quality.

Let's take a look at the following example:

```
func divide(x :Float, with y :Float)->Float { return x / y
}
```

This function is a very simple example. When we are running a test on this function with x = 4 and y = 2, and we are expecting the result to be 2, the test passes. The code coverage for this function is 100%. Does this mean we are fully covered and this is a bug-free code? Of course not. If we run another test on this function, when y = 0, we'll get an exception ("divided by zero").

It's a classic example of high coverage that doesn't mean bug-free code or even a high-quality code. It's just said that our tests hit many rows in our code when they run. There are also examples of companies and teams that were so passionate about high coverage that they created unit tests without any assertions, meaning their tests can never fail (!).

Another example is this:

```
func updateFirstName(newFirstName :String) { self.firstName =
newFirstName
}
```

A developer might create a test that runs this function with a parameter and then verify that the instance property named "firstName" received the new value. But since this function is so simple, it is clear that the developer is writing this test only to gain better code coverage.

The problem here is that when high code coverage is the target, developers prefer **quantity** over **quality**, and they become slaves of high numbers and statistics, instead of aiming for high quality and bug catching. It's easy in this case to just cover functions and move on with the code.

Also, we need to remember not all parts of our code are importantly equal, so investing the same effort in all your project areas is not a smart strategy. By testing the unimportant code, you might skip essential scenarios.

So Why Do We Need Code Coverage?

The fact that high code coverage doesn't necessarily mean "no bugs" doesn't mean it's useless. Code coverage is an excellent metric to **detect untested code**, and it's an excellent metric to identify areas of your app that are not covered or may contain bugs you are not aware of. It doesn't mean you need to cover them, but it gives you the full picture of your app.

Another issue that code coverage can help you is detecting dead code. If you see a private method that is not covered by tests, this could be a sign of unreachable code or, in other words, a "dead code." You can try checking the call hierarchy to track what functions call it and decide if you want to cover it or delete it if it's not in use.

And Then There Is Test Coverage. Wait. What?

When we say "Code Coverage," we mean "what is the percentage of our code that is covered by unit tests." Or, as mentioned before, if we have 50 lines of code and our tests execute 20 of them, we can tell that our code coverage is 40% (20 out of 50).

But there is another term – Test Coverage. A lot of teams and developers are confused by those two terms. While they may sound similar, they are not the same.

While code coverage measures the percentage of code covered by tests, Test Coverage measures the **percentage of requirements covered by tests**. Since test coverage doesn't deal with code but with requirements, it's less relevant for developers but more relevant to the QA testers. The reason I bring it here is that it can give you a sense of how to cover different aspects of your app and not just chasing code coverage metric or testing methods randomly.

So when we say "requirements," it is best practice to divide them into different groups that represent how our app is covered and tested in various aspects:

Product – What are the test coverage areas of your product? If your product contains ten features and tests cover only eight of them, we can say that in this case, you have a test coverage of 80%.

Risk – Your app requirements is a long list, that some of them are critical or blockers, and some of them are minor. Out of those that you define as critical and blockers, how many are covered? This is a crucial factor in understanding if your app is ready for production or not.

Parameter Value Coverage – Remember the example with the "divided by zero"? In main functions, you should test a vast scope of parameters. Of course, we have the usual suspects such as nil, 0, and "", but sometimes it's not enough. Try to focus on edge cases of user input – long texts, big arrays, and more.

Summary

We've learned how to incorporate tests in our daily work; we saw different mixes of test suites that we call "test pyramid," what are TDD and BDD, and what is code coverage and how it is covered.

As I said earlier, writing tests as part of your daily work is a professional challenge that is often related to culture and habits.

Another issue that is related to culture is running those tests automatically daily. This is a part of something called "continuous integration" and will be discussed in the next chapter.

CHAPTER 11

Using Command-Line Tools

The most important practice for continuous integration to work properly is frequent check-ins to trunk or mainline. You should be checking in your code at least a couple of times a day.

—David Farley

Introduction

While it's very convenient to use the Xcode UI interface to configure and run tests, it's impossible to do that when you want to run them on a remote server.

Fortunately, every new Xcode installed comes with a tool named "Xcode Command-Line Tools" to help you run your tests without any UI interface.

This chapter concludes the final piece in the puzzle by giving you the tools to integrate your great test suites into a continuous integration environment.

In this chapter, you will learn

1. What CI/CD means and how tests fit it

2. What are the command-line tools provided by Xcode

© Avi Tsadok 2020
A. Tsadok, *Pro iOS Testing*, https://doi.org/10.1007/978-1-4842-6382-2_11

3. Installing and setting up the xcodebuild application

4. How to run tests from the command line

5. How to run test plans from the command line

6. Exciting and useful xcodebuild features

What Is CI/CD Anyway?

"CI" and "CD" often come together – "CI/CD." However, these are two different processes:

CI (Continuous Integration) – In a continuous integration process, we take the code from all the developers/third party/server changes and **merge it together** to a new working build. The goal of this process is to make sure this build is stable and nothing broke along the way.

CD (Continuous Deployment) – In "Continuous Deployment," we upload the build to an online service and make sure we have an available app to download. In fact, CD is an **extension of the CI** process and cannot stand by itself.

How Tests Fit In?

Based on the preceding data, you can understand that tests are a central part of this process. In fact, a continuous integration without any tests involved is like dressing up, taking a babysitter, and going out to a restaurant for a glass of water – it just doesn't worth it.

There are plenty of tools that can help you integrate your tests automatically in a CI environment, but they all rely on Xcode command-line tools to run them.

Command-Line Tools

Command-Line tools are a great way to script your testing and incorporate it with CI/CD environments. They let you build, archive, and test your projects from the terminal command line and customize your run with different parameters and arguments.

Command-Line Tools are not just for CI/CD – they can also help you automate your tasks during development. For example, instead of repeating the same actions of testing different test plans, committing, and then archiving, you can implement all of that in one script file.

Meet xcodebuild

"xcodebuild" is the primary tool of the command-line tool package, and it's used to build, archive, and analyze test and any action you can do with the scheme.

The real power of xcodebuild is the flexibility to run various actions and configurations and, as a result of that, it is the primary tool for testing.

Install and Set Up xcodebuild

Although you can download Command-Line Tools separately, they come with every new Xcode.

But if you still want to download them, you have two options:

- Download from the Developer website.

- Install from the command line using xcode-select.

"xcode-select" is a command line that comes bundled with macOS. If you want to use it to install Command-Line Tools, open the Terminal and type

```
$ xcode-select -install
```

And press Enter.

Many developers have multiple versions of Xcode installed on their machine, and one of the first steps using xcodebuild is to make sure it works with the correct Xcode version.

To find out what is the "active" Xcode version, we can use xcode-select again for that:

```
$ xcode-select -p
/Applications/Xcode.app/Contents/Developer
```

To change the active Xcode version, locate the developer path and use the -switch command:

```
$ xcode-select -switch /Applications/Xcode12.app/Contents/
Developer
```

To uninstall Command-Line Tools, just delete /Library/Developer/ CommandLineTools with this command:

```
$ sudo rm -r /Library/Developer/CommandLineTools
```

Run Tests with xcodebuild

Running tests with xcodebuild is quite simple and requires very few parameters for the basic run. First, you need to make sure your current directory in the Terminal is the project directory.

A basic xcodebuild command looks something like this:

```
$ xcodebuild \
 -workspace MyWeatherApp.xcworkspace \
 -scheme MyWeatherApp \
 -destination 'platform=iOS Simulator,name=iPhone 11' \
 test
```

Let's go over the command parameters:

workspace – If you are using workspaces instead of projects (CocoaPods is a good example), pass your workspace name here.

scheme – Your selected scheme name.

test – Run the "test" action of the scheme.

destination – Specify the platform that is used for the test. A destination can be either a simulator or a physical device. Let's go deeper into this.

The Destination Argument

The syntax of the destination argument is based on key-value pairs. The first key is the **platform**, which describes whether it's a device or a simulator and what platform it is.

This is the list of platforms you can use:

- **OS X**, your Mac

- **iOS**, a connected iOS device

- **iOS Simulator**

- **watchOS**

- **watchOS Simulator**

- **tvOS**

- **tvOS Simulator**

The second key-value pair is related to the type of the device.

If it's a physical device, you can use either "**name**" to target the actual device name or "**id**" to target the device UUID.

If it's a simulator, the "name" key describes the name of the simulator ("iPhone 11"), and another key–value pair is "os" to specify the OS version ("11.0").

Let's see some examples:

To run your test on iPhone 11 Simulator, running iOS 12.0:

```
-destination "platform=iOS Simulator, name=iPhone 11, OS=12.0"
```

To run your test on a physical device:

```
-destination "platform=iOS, name=Avi's iPhone"
```

To list all of your available destinations, type in your terminal:

```
$ instruments -s devices
```

Run Test Plans from Command Line

You can use xcodebuild to run test plans right from the command line.

To see the list of available test plans for a scheme, use **showTestPlans** argument:

```
$ xcodebuild -scheme 'My Weather App' -showTestPlans
Test plans associated with the scheme "My Weather App":
        Localization Test Plan
        Memory
```

Running tests with a specific scheme will run the default test plan. To run a particular test plan, use **testPlan** argument:

```
$ xcodebuild \
 -workspace MyWeatherApp.xcworkspace \
 -scheme MyWeatherApp \
 -destination 'platform=iOS Simulator,name=iPhone 11' \
 -testPlan 'Memory' test
```

More xcodebuild Important Arguments

"xcodebuild" has more tricks up in its sleeves.

To list all the schemes, build configurations, and targets, use **list argument**:

```
$ xcodebuild -list
Information about project "My Weather App":
    Targets:
        My Weather App
        My Weather AppTests
        My Weather AppUITests

    Build Configurations:
        Debug
        Release

    If no build configuration is specified and -scheme is not
    passed then "Release" is used.

    Schemes:
        My Weather App
```

If you already build your app for testing and want to rerun tests without building it again, you can use **run-without-building** to save time:

```
$ xcodebuild \
  -workspace MyWeatherApp.xcworkspace \
  -scheme MyWeatherApp \
  -destination 'platform=iOS Simulator,name=iPhone 11' \
  run-without-building Test
```

On the other hand, if all you want is to build but not test, you can use **build-for-testing** argument:

```
$ xcodebuild \
 -workspace MyWeatherApp.xcworkspace \
 -scheme MyWeatherApp \
 -destination 'platform=iOS Simulator,name=iPhone 11' \
 build-for-testing Test
```

If you want to make sure Xcode cleans the project before running your tests, you can add **clean** to the command:

```
$ xcodebuild \
 clean \
 -workspace MyWeatherApp.xcworkspace \
 -scheme MyWeatherApp \
 -destination 'platform=iOS Simulator,name=iPhone 11' \
 test
```

To see all the available SDKs you can use, try the **showsdks** argument:

```
$ xcodebuild -showsdks
iOS SDKs:
        iOS 13.2                        -sdk iphoneos13.2

iOS Simulator SDKs:
        Simulator - iOS 13.2            -sdk iphonesimulator13.2

macOS SDKs:
        DriverKit 19.0                  -sdk driverkit.macosx19.0
        macOS 10.15                     -sdk macosx10.15

tvOS SDKs:
        tvOS 13.2                       -sdk appletvos13.2
```

```
tvOS Simulator SDKs:
        Simulator - tvOS 13.2          -sdk appletvsimulator13.2

watchOS SDKs:
        watchOS 6.1                     -sdk watchos6.1

watchOS Simulator SDKs:
        Simulator - watchOS 6.1         -sdk watchsimulator6.1
```

Summary

We've learned that it's not enough to write great tests; it's also essential to make sure to run them continuously. As an iOS developer, we need to focus on writing great software and solve complex problems. Let the automation server take care of running the tests for us.

Index

A

Arguments tab
  environment variables, 29, 30
  launch arguments
    Arguments Passed on
      Launch, 27
    code, 28, 29
    CommandLine, 28, 29
    list of arguments, 27, 28
    new argument, 27
    ProcessInfo, 28, 29
    user registration, 27
  scheme editor, 26
Arrange-Act-Assert (AAA), 120
Attachment, types, 215, 216

B

Baseline
  definition, 224
  deviation, 227
  info.plist, 237
  packet content, 237
  settings window, 225
  STDDEV, 226
  Xcode, 236, 238
Behavior-Driven Development
    (BDD), 270
declarative scenarios, 276
developer, 274
GHERKO language, 278
GIVEN section, 279, 280
multiple tests, 277
product owner, 273
QA, 273
real-world data, 277
registration screen, 275
TDD process, 274
technical issue, 273
THEN section, 278
use cases, 273
user scenarios, 275, 276
Black Box testing, 131, 132, 134
Bottom-Up Approach
    (BUA), 123, 128
Bugs, 263

C

CalendarService method, 127
Classic pyramid, 264, 265
Clean Code, 144
  DRY, 146
  KISS, 145, 146
  pleasant to read, 147
  pleasant to write, 148
  YAGNI, 147

U

Y, Z

Printed in the United States
by Bookmasters

Printed in the United States
By Bookmasters